SENDING THE ELEVATOR BACK DOWN

WHAT WE'VE LEARNED FROM GREAT WOMEN IN COMPLIANCE

by LISA FINE
and MARY SHIRLEY

Sending the Elevator Back Down: What We've Learned from Great Women in Compliance is published by CCI Press, an imprint of CCI Media Group, Dallas, Texas

ISBN: 978-1-7350285-1-4

Editor: Emily Ellis

Designer: Sam Kerner

Author Photo: Tracey Salazar Photography

CCI Media Group

www.corporatecomplianceinsights.com

CONTENTS

Acknowledgements

My parents always talked about the importance of giving us "roots and wings." I have always felt that I have both unconditional love and support from my parents and also the ability to fly. My dad, Bob, gave me his love for the law and reasoning, and I feel so fortunate to be able to share that with him. My mom, Eileen, is a teacher and librarian who is always there for family and friends. She is always willing to help people in need with grace and kindness and without ever making them feel obligated to her; it's a quality I hope I can emulate. My sister, Julie Fine, is my #1 cheerleader and best friend. She's a great reporter and political analyst, and she has a great sense of humor and an even bigger heart. My roots are strong because of them.

Mary Shirley, thank you. You were my first compliance friend, and you brought me into this community. I had no idea we would become partners-in-compliance, podcast co-hosts, and very dear friends.

I am so grateful for my friends who are my family (you know who you are) and the people who support me every day. I am so lucky. A few need an extra mention, as they have been dear friends and professional sounding boards for too long: Kris Brown, my work spouse for life, and who helped me find my professional path; Chris Farmer, the brother I never had, and who both supports me and helps me do better every day; Jennifer Antolini Bradner, my first friend in law school, and who is still a rock and my favorite ski buddy (with the exception of her children); and Stacey Dansky, for always being there at the exact moment I needed encouragement or a good laugh.

Lastly, thank you to the contributors to this book and the Great Women in Compliance podcast community. Whenever I hear from someone on LinkedIn or get emails or read comments, I feel honored, flattered, and thrilled to be part of a group who are working so diligently to make this profession, our organizations, and our world better every day.

Lisa Fine

I would like to gratefully acknowledge my late father, Keith, who lived every day guided by a strong ethical compass and doing right by others; my beautiful mother, Mable, whose formidable intellect is ever-in-spiring; and my ever-supportive brother, Kieran, a fellow expat exploring the world.

I express my deepest appreciation for the women and men in the compliance community, who have supported Lisa's and my endeavours to advance and empower women in compliance, as well as my dear friends outside of the field, who have nevertheless cheered us on from the sidelines.

I wish to pay tribute to the women who gave of their time and expertise and who opened up their hearts to us all to contribute to this book. You are phenomenal, and it is our pleasure to know you and include your insights.

To you, our reader: Your time and attention is such valuable real estate, and I'm thrilled and so appreciative that you chose this book to keep you company. Whenever you feel isolated or alone in your role, I hope you'll pull out this book and be reminded of all of the Great Women in Compliance who stand beside you and want you to succeed.

Mary Shirley

Introduction

There is debate as to whether Queen Bee syndrome, also known as being "mean girls" in the office, is really a thing. First documented by psychologists in 1973, Queen Bee syndrome describes the behavior of women who, when in positions of power or authority, treat female subordinates worse simply because they are women. Maybe it's difficult for these women to accept that paving the way for others should be seen as a positive. After all, they fought tooth and nail to establish and earn their success despite gender barriers. Why should anyone after them get a free ride?

But the typical dog-eat-dog workplace is competitive enough without women sabotaging each other. Anecdotally, we've both observed that the nicest and most successful people are also the ones most willing to help others achieve their full potential and aspirations.

Both inside and outside of compliance, we notice that truly successful people tend to be generous with their knowledge, support, enthusiasm, and praise. When someone else has an accomplishment, they are the first to champion and congratulate.

When compared to Queen Bees, we know there are far more givers, mentors, and sponsors in the compliance world, so we were hopeful that when we solicited submissions for a book to encourage the next generation of Great Women in Compliance, we would receive truly valuable pieces of advice, along with stories of strength, ambition, and generally being badass.

When we put out the call for contributors, we knew we wanted to create something different from a typical book on compliance focused on regulations, case analysis, and the substantive and serious "hard skills" that benefit this profession. Instead, we envisaged women all over the world coming together to share triumphs and truths about facing cross-cultural challenges and adversity.

We hoped the submissions would be emotive, vulnerable, uplifting, inspiring, and perhaps even raw. Boy, did the compliance community deliver.

What follows is a collection of experiences that reveal hard-earned accomplishments, lessons that were learned at a price, personally confronting moments, and that sweet spot where true character is made and displayed.

In this book, women of astounding professional merit and capability kick off their shoes, sit back, and give us straight-up real talk. It's refreshing, it's human, and most of all, it's deeply relatable.

You'll feel like you're at home, comfortably relaxed with a glass of wine (pinot noir, if you're like Lisa, or cup of hot water with lemon and honey, if you're like Mary) while surrounded by a group of close friends. Here, title does not matter, and there is no in-group. We simply delight in the intimacy, familiarity, and, at times, catharsis that comes from sharing our growth and the moments that shaped who we are today.

The advice, reassurance, and cautionary tales offered here form a gift for others in the community to unwrap and apply to their own career paths and personal lives. Writing, reading, and sharing these words is but one way many of the contributors help the compliance community by sending the elevator back down.

Sending the elevator back down is one of our favorite themes, and perhaps unsurprisingly, it's one of the most explicit of the common traits we have identified in our experience as co-hosts of the Great Women in Compliance Podcast. So many of the women we encounter tirelessly give back to the compliance community and give others a leg up where they can.

So what does sending the elevator back down really mean? It is derived from a Jack Lemmon quote: "I believe if you have been successful at what you dreamed of doing with your life, then it is your obligation to spend a good portion of your time sending the elevator back down."

This stems from advice Jack Lemmon gave to other actors, and we think it's a pretty solid principle to live by. If you have achieved a certain level of success, we encourage you to think about how you can pay it forward by helping others achieve their goals as well. It is an excellent way to pay tribute to the trailblazing women who came before us, paving the way and breaking through barriers that helped us get where we are. There is still a lot of work to do, of course. We think our cumulative efforts will continue to move the dial.

One of the reasons we set up the Great Women in Compliance Podcast and associated community page on LinkedIn was to give back to the compliance community. We wanted to put a spotlight on the remarkable achievements of women in ethics and compliance, provide a platform to showcase their thought leadership and innovations, and create a space for knowledge sharing, education, and inspiration. There also have been many ancillary benefits, such as building our own networks and facilitating introductions and new relationships between our listeners and guests. We hope these efforts will encourage listeners to keep cheering on other women, to engage in active learning and professional development, and to challenge others to join them in banding together for the collective benefit of all women in compliance.

If you think you're not yet in a position to send the elevator back down, remember this: it's human nature to think you first need to have "made it" in order to give back. **The reality is, everyone has something to offer; it need not be substantive. You may think you have nothing to offer someone more senior than you, but that's not true.** For folks with more limited experience and influence, there are ways you can help propel other women forward and amplify their voices.

If you'd like to acknowledge someone who has helped you, then send the elevator back up, if you will. An easy way to do this is to take photos of that person speaking at a conference and do a social media post with your top takeaways from the session. Or you can simply send the photo to the person for their own social media post or to share with family members who may wonder what they get up to at these mysterious compliance conferences.

The point is, like the subject of the book *Charlie and the Great Glass Elevator*, you have the power to send the elevator in any direction you choose. Applaud the thought leadership, critical analysis, or desirable behavior of other women (and men) publicly – whether it be in the office, on social media, or in a personal note of encouragement. It's always appreciated. It does not matter whether you're at the top of your profession or just starting out. Everyone gains joy, confidence, and fulfillment from knowing they've made a difference. Write them a message to let them know how the lessons you've learned from them have impacted you personally and how this has positively affected your development personally and professionally.

Through these stories, we hope to encourage you to be a Great Woman in Compliance and send the elevator in any direction you choose. When women support other women, all of our boats collectively rise. Remember, as James Keller said, "a candle loses nothing by lighting another candle."

The Authors

Chapter One

I Knew I Had Made It When...

Mary says...

“ Compliance seems to attract a certain type of person. We value fairness, justice and doing the right thing. As **Beth Colling** points out elsewhere in the book, we are often natural rule followers.

Another characteristic typical of compliance folk is that we have different interpretations of "making it," depending on who we are and what we value. What success looks like depends on your vantage point. Success doesn't necessarily mean standing at the highest point of the ladder, though of course that's the measurement of "making it" for some.

It is, therefore, unsurprising that the following stories highlight a sense of self-achievement when these Great Women in Compliance followed their instincts, contributed to their communities, and came to understand the role they play as a key cog within a larger machine serving a wider purpose.

Sometimes, knowing you've made it just means that you feel you're on the right track—even though the final destination may remain unknown.

We celebrate the contributors in this chapter for their commitment to ethical workplaces and the compliance community. Had Lisa Fine not actively reached out, as she describes later in this chapter, in an effort to build her network, the Great Women in Compliance Podcast would never have been born.

To you who are inspired by these stories, we say: Keep making the most of your abilities and you will continue to reinvent "making it" for a long time to come.

"

Courage Under Fire

As **Marcy Maslov** notes, being successful in ethics and compliance sometimes requires courage.

"I've faced the wrong end of the barrel of a gun for cleaning up unethical and illegal behavior," she says. "I did not feel great after most of these experiences, I can tell you."

In her long career she has stared down supervisors, CEOs, colleagues, and even friends. She recalls being the lone voice brave enough to label an action as unethical and refusing to participate in an activity, knowing it might cost her the job.

The light bulb finally came on the day I learned my efforts had helped turn around a manufacturing plant from the worst to the best in productivity, and that the girls in this facility now light a candle for me every Christmas in gratitude for my saving them from being raped.

I thought I'd failed in that job. There was nothing in the corporate handbook guiding me on what to do, so I followed my own standards. I stood up for my ethical values and put my career with the company at risk to protect these girls and "do the right thing." I ended up leaving that job because I could no longer trust the people I worked with and for.

It was my first real-life lesson that not everyone has the same standards that I do, and it set me on my path to entering the ethics and compliance world many years later. I was just living my life and being true to myself. It took many years after I'd left this job to truly recognize the value of my effort. A simple phone call from a colleague helped me see the true impact of my efforts. And it keeps me going even in the face of extreme pressure today.

Marcy Maslov
Chief Integrity Builder
Phoenix, Arizona

Meeting People Where They Are

Extreme pressure is part of the job description, whether in the trenches in the office or when representing an employer abroad. **Gwendolyn Hassan** knows a thing or two about international travel, having been an exchange student in her school days and later, as a young lawyer, when she looked for every opportunity to immerse herself in the traditions, foods, and dialects of other countries. She eagerly raised her hand for every project or deal that would land her on foreign soil and give her the opportunity to combine her compliance practice with her love of languages and cultures.

A company I once worked for had a particular location in South America that was a proverbial "black hole." We had never received a helpline report from the location and had no regular dialogue with local management. I pitched the idea of doing a short local "residency," spending a week on-site with no specific agenda while working alongside the local team each day and making myself available.

While my management wasn't entirely convinced of the value of such a residency (I believe the term "boondoggle" was mentioned at one point), I successfully "sold" the idea based on my ability to speak the local language and my fervent belief that only by spending time with the local team could we really gain insight into why the culture there appeared to be so closed.

I made the trip, set myself up in a small conference room, and walked around introducing myself to everyone I could. I ate local cuisine in the employee cafeteria, and I literally hung around the company water cooler and looked for every opportunity to get to know people. I was approachable and available, and on my fourth day there, an employee stopped by and asked if I had time to go for a walk.

The employee had heard through the grapevine that "a friendly woman from compliance" was here for the week and that I spoke the local language.

We walked around the grounds of our facility and chatted for almost an hour in Spanish. They described a facility culture of silence, where employees were discouraged from speaking up, instructed not to use the helpline in order to hide issues from the corporate office, and where employees had a very real fear of retaliation. The employee provided details of multiple significant potential compliance issues along with the names of other employees who wanted to speak with me while I was on-site. In fact, the employee told me they had been "waiting" for someone they could talk to who wasn't beholden to local leadership.

I spent the rest of that day and all of the next talking in Spanish with other employees who voiced the same concerns. As a result of my week in residency, the company not only discovered and resolved what could have been multiple costly compliance issues, but was also able to implement a number of local culture initiatives, including specific interventions to incentivize helpline reporting and address the fear of retaliation.

By "being there" on-site, speaking the local language, and simply being available to listen, I had "made it." It was when I first realized that the highest use of my talents lay in combining my passions and that doing so was of great value not only to me, but also to the companies I work for.

Gwendolyn Lee Hassan
Director & Managing Counsel, Global Compliance
Oak Park, Illinois

"

Developing an ethical culture in any organization is really no different from what is required to build a house. You need a strong foundation to ensure the integrity of the structure. Key foundational pillars that are often overlooked are emotional intelligence and empathy; they help open doors to building trust, create open lines of communication, and aid in eliciting candor and honesty.

I have learned that connecting on a personal level before focusing on compliance-related issues or concerns is critical in forming a bond of trust. I make it a point to learn more about a person's cultural values and personal interests. There is something to be said about putting yourself in someone else's shoes, connecting with them on a deeper level, and effectively communicating and resolving conflicting viewpoints without tension or resistance. In this way, stakeholders are more likely to consult with me to resolve an ethical dilemma and act with integrity. It is at this point I know with confidence that the house I built is sound.

Tiffany A. Archer
Regional Ethics & Compliance Officer / Corporate
Counsel (Americas/Europe)
New York, New York

"

A Seat at the Table

Margarita Derelanko says "the smallest fleeting moment at work not only can confirm you've chosen the right path, but also can shape your mission and your professional *why*."

Here's the story of her moment.

It was a Thursday morning meeting in which cross-functional leadership came together, post-merger, to demo a new electronic health record vendor. At this point in the organizational cycle, the compliance department had been established and well-known after a few years of compliance awareness and engagement campaigns. Merger partners had also had opportunities to engage with us, their compliance teammates, and learn about the mission and elements of the program. I knew that the proactive culture of compliance had been firmly infused into operations and co-workers' minds, pre-merger, and that it had also been making its way toward those less familiar with our compliance department, post-merger.

In that meeting, I made a conscious decision to observe and note whether someone from the leadership team would ask compliance-related questions from the vendor (and if you are reading this book, you may very well know that this decision does not come easy to us compliance practitioners).

By then, the compliance department had been receiving a steady stream of inquiries from both leadership and front-line teammates who did not shy away from using PHI, BAA, and other compliance acronyms in their correspondence. I had also been told that compliance was discussed during meetings even when the compliance team was not in the room. So I decided to let it unfold.

Minutes into the demo, someone behind me raised a question: "Is this platform HIPAA-compliant? Is it secure?" Later, another voice asked, "What about segregation of records?" The compliance questions continued. The voices were familiar to me, as they were program managers and mid-managers that my department had been partnering with for years.

I smiled. I was filled with pride, knowing that compliance was important to those leaders and that they felt comfortable asking difficult questions and using compliance terminology.

In that moment, I realized that I want to be remembered professionally for helping organizations integrate compliance into the work and minds of teammates by making it attainable, operational, and engaging. I felt that I had made a difference and helped leadership and their programs be better versions of themselves, using compliance as a tool. That was the beginning of my beautiful journey of fully discovering my professional *why*, which brought me to doing what I love with my new work family.

You know you've "made it" when compliance is on your co-workers' minds and when they think of you as a business partner and resource.

How often do you let your colleagues "speak compliance" on your behalf? Have you ever observed what happens when you let someone else speak up? You may be surprised!

How you get to this feeling that your compliance program "made it" (even on a small scale) may differ. However, I bet that if you establish your compliance brand, focus on training, and genuinely engage your gatekeepers and front-line teammates, over time, you will nurture compliance advocates in your organization who may be just as comfortable saying, "We need a BAA because there is PHI," making you feel so proud...

Margarita Derelanko
Director of Compliance
Williamstown, New Jersey

"

"I knew I made it when… I was the only woman in the room discussing an urgent client situation with our CEO and several top executives. I quickly realized that not only did I understand what had led to the urgent situation, I knew how to solve it. I explained the problem and solution. When the CEO agreed and asked "who is the best person to deliver the message?," I did not hesitate to say it was me. I remember walking out of the small office and thinking that the resolution of this issue could make or break my career. Luckily, it all worked out—I met with the client, resolved their concerns, and gained the trust of our leaders."

Michelle Beistle
Chief Ethics, Compliance & Privacy Officer
Fairfax, Virginia

Now, to Pay it Forward

Lisa says...

" When I started in my first non-law-firm corporate role, I felt fortunate to get the opportunity to work in HR compliance. I remember a steep learning curve, but soon realized I had found a "home" in the ethics and compliance area.

Not only was I completely engaged with the subject matter, I loved the opportunity to work with people in all areas of the business and all over the world to make sure they thought about ethical decisions and regulations.

Although sometimes compliance can be a lonely profession, I soon realized that while it could feel lonely at an organization, there is a community of ethics and compliance professionals out there. I just had to find them.

My first conference was in Chicago. Not only was I thrilled to meet so many people who were excited about things I wanted to do, I also met Mary Shirley. After hearing one of her presentations, I knew she was fantastic, but I did not know how much our paths would cross.

This was the beginning of me building my compliance network.

Fast-forward a few years: Suddenly, talking about things like Department of Justice Guidelines, GDPR, and so many compliance-related acronyms was second nature, and I was in a new job. When I was meeting new people at work and working on new projects, I realized I was also building a network of resources through this group of people who were now friends as well as colleagues.

Over the past year, people I've met have said they listen to the podcast or they've heard me speak, and it makes me feel like I'm making an impact. Even better, I'm now in the position of bringing people into my network and can help others as people have done for me—all while doing substantive work with great people in my job.

I don't know if that means "I made it," because there is always more to do. But these accomplishments have helped me grow and continue to evolve as an ethics and compliance professional. "Making it," in my opinion, is what you "make of it." Being able to become a leader, keep learning, and pay it forward seems like as good a definition of success as anything. **"**

Chapter Two

The Only Woman in the Room

Lisa says...

" My first memory of being the only woman in the room was not in a boardroom or with the senior team. It was in a workshop with men who were senior in the operations of the organization and who also worked long hours in a manufacturing-type unit. (While not the only woman in the room, I was one of just a few; I was, however, the only woman lawyer and compliance professional.)

Needless to say, they were a little wary of this well-intentioned lady who showed up, and I was very aware of being female and corporate and having zero operations experience. I had been in my job for one month, and there were many acronyms being thrown around that day.

Early on, the most senior operations leader started asking me what each acronym meant, which was well-intentioned, and it started to become a running joke. It was intimidating. I channeled the wisdom of **Kristy Grant-Hart**, authored below, and decided to make sure my voice was heard on my own terms, and to speak out regularly so that being quizzed about acronyms would not be the only time I was in the spotlight.

Finally the moment came when I knew the answer (I had learned the particular acronym in an investigation, but I didn't mention that). I answered correctly, and all the men applauded.

We all learn from our experiences, and as a white American woman, I think a lot about how I am perceived, the barriers and challenges I have, and how these things impact both how I communicate and how I respond. I am also aware that my challenges differ from those of women of color and women from different countries of origin who might not be speaking in her first language. I try to learn from those experiences. Being the only woman in the room is different for each of us, but as you'll see in the stories shared below, our diversity is something to be celebrated. **"**

When Your Knees Are Shaking Under the Table, Smile

Breathe, I said to myself. *No, seriously. Breathe, or you're going to pass out.*

The first time I was scheduled to present at a board meeting, I felt weak, sickly, and out of place. I felt like an impostor. What sort of silly misunderstanding had led to me presenting to this room of (mostly) men who were supposed to take what I had to say seriously?

I've had that queasy feeling repeatedly in my career, from the law firm I worked at—where 85% of the partners were men—all the way until today, when I frequently work with and sell to men at the highest levels of business.

For me, some of the best techniques to manage this anxiety are physical actions I can take. Research proves that our physical body sends messages to our mind based on how we are sitting, standing, or smiling. By manipulating our bodies, we can change our experience of the world. How does this work in practice? My favorite techniques are to:

Sit Confidently at the Table. According to Facebook CEO Sheryl Sandberg (and my own experience), many women shrink back and wait to take a seat until the men are seated at a meeting, or sit on the side of the room instead of at the table. When you enter a room, choose a seat at the table and act like you belong there. People will take their cues from you. If you act like you belong there, you will.

Take Up Space. Women are often taught to be small, both physically and with their demands. Instead of crossing your arms and hiding in the chair, boldly place your elbows on the table and take up space. By simply sitting up straight and using open body language, you'll send a signal that you are supposed to be in the room and are confident of your place.

Commit to Speaking at Least Once. Women frequently don't feel like they have anything "important enough" to say to interrupt the flow of conversation. If the room is heated or people are disagreeing, it can be very intimidating to insert your ideas or opinion. When you go into an important meeting, challenge yourself to speak up at least once. It can be intimidating, but remember: Not everything the other people are saying is brilliant. By adding to the conversation, you're raising points other people might not have made, which adds value. By adding value, you're much more likely to be invited back.

First In? Stay Standing. If you're the first person in the room, stay standing until someone else joins, at which point, welcome him or her in and then sit down when they do. By standing and welcoming the second person in, you're subtly signalling that this is your room, and that you are welcoming them into your space.

Channel Your Inner Sasha Fierce. Beyoncé has an alter ego she calls "Sasha Fierce." Sasha walks with a swagger, owns the room, and isn't afraid of anyone. When you're feeling small or frightened, it can be helpful to develop your own alter ego or to simply act as if you're the confident woman you want to be. Acting as if something is true and then physically embodying that experience sends hormones to your brain that reinforce what you are acting out. You'll quickly find that by embodying who you'd like to be, you begin to find your inner confidence.

I'd love to say that I've overcome fear and can present without discomfort. I doubt that I will ever feel confident all the time, but that's why I've got my inner Madonna. She's not afraid of anything, and when I embody her, neither am I.

Kristy Grant-Hart
CEO and former Chief Compliance Officer
Fayetteville, West Virginia

> Be true to your beliefs and trust your instincts. Like many women, I experienced sexual harassment in my early twenties. While my friends will say I'm a strong person, I wasn't back then. So, here's my advice: When you are faced with an experience that doesn't feel right, it probably isn't right. Follow your gut. Speak up and don't apologize.

M. Beth Colling
Senior Vice President and Chief Compliance Officer
Boston, Massachusetts

Walk Like a (Wo)man

It's not so rare that, in professional settings, I'm the only woman in the room, and one of only a few Latinas in a leadership position in a radius of several miles (especially in Indiana).

As women strive for leadership positions, exercising our authority and making our voices, ideas, and opinions heard in a room full of people may feel really uncomfortable.

It's very common to fall into the trap of emulating the way men lead. Lack of representation of women leaders around you may do that to you.

Learn how to recognize this trap before you fall into it, and find your own management style. Whether you are assertive and vocal, an introvert who gets things done, or a mix of both, your leadership style should mirror who you are as a person.

Emulating leadership styles from men leaders around you won't do that for you, and it becomes tiring, because it's simply not who you are. Believe me, I tried that and failed miserably. Only when I recognized what worked for my leadership style did I become able to lead with authenticity and be more efficient as a leader.

Fernanda Beraldi
Senior Director, Ethics & Compliance
Indianapolis, Indiana

Be Authentic. When I was a brand-new compliance lawyer and walked into a room of senior leaders, I was so intent on sounding like an expert and impressing my clients that I may have seemed more like a "compliance lawyer robot" than Rebecca Walker. But in those moments when I let "me" slip into the discussion, that's when I really connected with others and was able to lobby for the compliance program most effectively.

I recall one important meeting in particular—a number of years ago—with a client's senior leadership team at which I was the only woman in the room. My computer was hooked up to a screen, and I was delivering my remarks rather stiffly, when I pushed the wrong button and a photo of my three kids appeared. My face turned red and I was mortified, but I managed to jokingly introduce the group to my "junior associates" and get back to the PowerPoint. However, in that moment of being a mom, I was able to create a level of engagement that I think I would not have achieved if I hadn't made that error.

Rebecca Walker
Compliance Lawyer
Santa Monica, California

Panting for Change

Sometimes we are the only women in the room because the field is dominated by men. At other times, we aren't outnumbered exactly, but find ourselves still standing out. This was the case for **Sandra Erez**, who prides herself on doing things a little differently. Evidently, it's a lifelong trait!

In a light-hearted story Sandra shares from her younger years, she recalls a seemingly small choice—breaking dress code—as feeling practically historic in the moment. Even small moments can be formative, for us and our female peers.

It is a sultry June evening in 1971 in the Long Island suburbs of New York, and I am poised to parade down the aisle in my elementary school graduation ceremony. I glanced enviously at my classmates, boys slick-haired and crammed into their suits, girls decked in frilly pastel dresses, tapping out a nervous staccato rhythm with their dress shoes. They look back at me, giving me the once-over with a mixture of pity and wonder reflected in their incredulous eyes.

I flash them a fake brave smile, wondering if they can hear the pounding of my heart over the crackly noises spilling out over the faulty PA system.

On cue, the solemn notes of "Pomp and Circumstance" fill the air, snapping me out of my reverie and imposing the gravity of the occasion on the waiting crowd. As we shuffle forward toward the podium, I start to panic that I have made a huge mistake, and my eyes dart to the auditorium's emergency exits as I consider making a run for it. But locked into position like a shackled prisoner between my fellow inmates, I have no choice but to keep moving forward until I am in full view of the firing squad.

There is a murmured hush from the stunned audience of school superintendents, principals, teachers, and parents as I gingerly make my way onto the stage. At the podium, I am frozen like a deer in the headlights, my bold flouting of convention causing the stern principal's smile to fade like a crease under a hot iron. Deafening silence filled the hallowed hall as I stretched out my hand to receive my diploma, the first girl in 46 years to break strict school dress code and wear PANTS—jeans, at that!

Time stood still as I waited for the sound and fury of the System to rain down on me, replacing the smattering of applause dutifully rewarded to each graduate.

As I held my breath, I recalled a sweaty Kathrine Switzer, triumphant at the finish line as one of the first women to run a "man's race" in the 1967 Boston Marathon.

Too young to burn my bra (I didn't wear one yet) but swept up in the tide of social change, I was eager to challenge the status quo of blatant inequality between the sexes. Like Neil Armstrong's moon landing two years prior, I had stuck my trousered flag between the ancient pocked floorboards, boring one small hole into the thickly laid foundation of male dominance.

Waiting for the referee to make the call, I spotted my teacher clutching at her pearls and almost stretching them beyond their breaking point. I think I remember hoping they would burst free like a volley of shots into the assembled crowd, something I myself wanted to do.

Abruptly, as if in the aftermath of a summer cloudburst, the charged atmosphere de-electrified. The school superintendent's stormy face crinkled into an acquiescent smile, and as he thrust out a black-suited arm offering my diploma, my heart swelled with victory.

And for all of us young women in the room at that time, this authoritative gesture was akin to the green flag at Nascar announcing the commencement of the long race ahead.

Sandra Erez
Director of Global Compliance
Jerusalem, Israel

The Only "Young Woman" in the Room

If you are a young woman who is a compliance manager in an environment dominated by male leaders, these tips from **Maria Monica Morris** will be particularly valuable for you. She bases them on personal experiences where, generally speaking, the male leaders were not used to having a woman—much less, a young one—take part in the decision-making process.

Senior management support is essential and everyone must know about it. Successful compliance programs must have senior management support. This isn't news. However, senior management sometimes fails to make that support known to regional and local managers. It is not enough to express support in company policies or in once-a-year funding decisions. It must be expressed in writing and orally, constantly, and in formal and informal settings. Senior management's failure to support the compliance function can diminish the authority and credibility of compliance managers.

In contrast, when senior management communicates their support in this fashion, managers will know that they must listen to the compliance manager, regardless of her age or gender. Imagine how different a regional manager will react to a young female compliance manager's advice if the CEO personally calls him and tells him that he must work together with her.

Identify allies and team up with them. For a young woman in a managerial role, a key challenge is being heard and taken into account by other leaders. One way for compliance managers to make significant contributions to a company is by engaging others in the same mission. Finance, human resources, and senior management are usually good allies for compliance managers. These allies are valuable for many reasons. Many times, they are the ones who will get the compliance manager involved in meetings and in issues that she would not otherwise know about. This is particularly valuable when stakeholders underestimate the compliance manager for being a young woman and don't think she should be in the room.

Additionally, allies' interests are usually aligned with those of compliance. A finance chief will want to make sure the company complies with anti-corruption regulations to safeguard the company's financial reputation. A practical way to win powerful allies is to identify who the stakeholders and gatekeepers are, meet up with them for coffee, and regularly keep them apprised of what compliance is working on. This helps build relationships with key employees and get people to trust you.

Keep a paper trail of in-person interactions. Occasionally, managers verbally agree or commit to do something the compliance manager has asked for. This may feel as if the manager is just saying "yes" to simply appease compliance. It is crucial to record these types of interactions in writing to create accountability. A quick and polite way to do this is to send a follow-up email to the manager after the interaction, summarizing what was agreed upon. The email should be written in a way that does not require a response. If they do not agree with you, they will likely let you know. This email will create accountability and facilitate future follow-ups.

Call out gender and age bias. One way to stop bias is by calling it out. I've been called bossy many times, behind my back and to my face. Once, I was told that I should be more "diplomatic" and "less bossy" in the way I spoke to a male manager. The next time I had to meet with that manager, I decided to address the bias in a humorous way. Before I gave my opinions or recommendations, I would start by saying "I don't mean to sound bossy," followed by a gracious laugh. This approach worked and, after some time, this manager became an excellent ally.

Maria Monica Morris
Latin-American Compliance & Investigations Counsel
Bogota, Colombia

"

An executive meeting I was attending for the first time started with a senior executive asking every participant (there were twenty-five to thirty people in the room) to show the orange-colored cloth they were wearing that day; it was a company color. I did not know about this practice, and then it was my turn to answer. I said that I do have orange on me (thinking about a tiny stripe on my socks). But to my surprise, the executive asked me to show what exactly was orange, which I refused, saying you need to trust your compliance officer. The next second, the room was full of giggles and laughter. Apparently, the room full of men hadn't thought about socks as an option …

Elena Kovaleva
Compliance Officer
Dubai, UAE

Gravitas is Earned in Moments of Grit

I have met with a four-star general and his entourage in a Middle Eastern country and questioned his compliance with our policies. I have had to terminate many folks due to their poor judgment and lack of integrity. I have also had very frank conversations with folks in the C-suite, telling them that unless they took action immediately, they would be labeled as a sycophant.

In all these instances, I was the only female in the room. Those societal stereotypes and beliefs or expectations that you can easily be persuaded seem to be magnified when you're a female in an authoritative role. Comments such as "you should smile more," or passive-aggressive chuckles when you confront someone who is not being compliant happen all too often.

The most important thing I learned with these experiences was that gravitas is acquired in moments of grit.

I walked into each situation, sometimes nervous, panicky, or apoplectic, but always knowing my responsibility to the organization. Oftentimes, they tried to make me feel like I did not belong in the room. In some cases, I had to deal with an instigator, someone who pushed all my buttons; an intimidator, who literally tried to be the biggest person in the room; or, my least favorite, a disingenuous person, who said everything they thought I wanted to hear just to get me *out* of the room.

Again, the remedy for all of this is knowing what you were hired to do. As compliance professionals, our sole purpose is to ensure the company's policies, its procedures, and all applicable laws and regulations are being adhered to. We are an essential part of the organization, and it is our job to identify and mitigate any risk to the organization.

Tell yourself you do belong there; show it in your expressions, in your body language, and in your wisdom. Know your stuff when you walk in the room. Always be prepared.

Step into moments of discomfort and use your grit to gain your gravitas.

Vuslat Eksi
Ethics & Compliance Officer
Washington, D.C.

"

Do not let your vision interfere with stereotypes! Understanding your values is key in achieving your vision. Having said that, I remember when I—just turned 30—promised myself that I would always stand up and speak out for my own values and integrity.

No matter our gender, race, religion, etc., we are always seen through the lenses of stereotypes. Speaking up about these circumstances supports younger generations as well as peers, and from what I have witnessed, it also makes older generations think.

Isn't this what we want to achieve? Making people think about their stereotypes? If we are not breaking the taboo and standing out by being a role model, nothing will change.

Sonja Stirnimann
CEO
Switzerland

"

Be Seen—And Heard

I'm always amazed by the propensity of women, especially young women, to self-marginalize physically. I can't tell you how many times I've walked into a conference room and seen women sitting along the periphery, rather than at the table. Or I'll walk into a conference or seminar and see women sitting at the back of the room. As far as I'm concerned, if you don't take a literal seat at the table, you will never get a figurative seat at it. So, belly up to that table, sit up straight, and engage. You deserve to be there as much as anyone else in that room.

When it comes to being heard, I don't mean volume. (Which is ironic coming from me, since I'm one of the loudest people in any room.) It's important to have a voice. Note that I'm not advocating talking just for the sake of talking. Have something meaningful to say. Make it a point to speak at least once on every conference call and video chat and in every meeting you attend (and more than once, if the event is looooong). That means you have to be prepared for every meeting and engaged in every discussion. Conference calls and meetings are absolutely not the time to multitask or be absorbed in your mobile device. Be alert, pay attention, understand the topic, form an opinion, offer solutions, and, in general, speak up. To this day, I challenge current colleagues of my own vintage to do the same.

Andrea Falcione
Principal & Head of Advisory Services
Boston, Massachusetts

When I am the only woman in the room, which has been all too often, I try not to be the only one in the room that doesn't speak. I am in the room for a reason and have worked hard to have a voice. Thus, I take being the only woman in the room as an obligation to speak up in a thoughtful and contributory way. Undoubtedly, when I am the only woman in the room, I see at least one or two things differently than the men—from a different angle or a risk that they have not considered. So, in turn, my perspective reminds others in the room of the value of a woman's opinion and the diversity it offers.

Asha Palmer
Chief Ethics & Compliance Officer
Montclair, New Jersey

Overcoming Bias

When navigating gender politics, choose a style that is true for you. There are lots of successful women with a variety of styles. Be true to yourself. You won't feel right if you adopt someone else's style; it won't be comfortable or natural. Research suggests that even when women adopt stereotypical male behaviors in the workforce (i.e., confidence, golfing, etc.), we are judged negatively anyway!

This is doubly the case for women like me: visible minorities.

Try to build a strong network of people you trust inside and outside your organization—especially with women and other minority groups. They can help you assess the discrimination you may be experiencing and assist with strategies to improve the situation in your organization, or cope until you are able to leave.

Never listen to anyone who says "it's all in your head," especially if you are in a place where the culture is unlikely to change. The risk with believing "it's all in my head" is that it erodes your confidence, which will undermine you even further and create more obstacles for you.

It's possible to have a lot of success in the environments where you are the only woman in the room, especially when you are the trailblazer paving the way for other women. But to ignore the stress caused by systemic sexism or racism in the workforce is to bear a burden that should be shared by the leadership of the organization.

Amee Sandhu
CEO, Founder & Principal Lawyer
Toronto, Ontario, Canada

Chapter Three

Lessons Learned ... the Hard Way

" Like embarrassing moments, lessons learned the hard way afford us an opportunity to grow personally and professionally, but at a cost: a boatload of discomfort.

It takes a special person to be humble enough to admit to a mistake and an insightful person to figure out the root cause and how it can be avoided in the future. In this chapter, I especially commend **Kris Robidoux**'s recount of a particularly difficult time. Reading her contribution gave me goosebumps. It took a Great Woman in Compliance to land on her feet after such a challenging experience. Kris, it makes us love you even more!

I've always loved the idea that imperfection is what actually makes a person perfect. The little flaws are so relatable. The person who overcomes adversity and corrects their mistakes? You're practically the underdog in your own story!

There is an unattributed saying: "A smart (wo)man learns from [her] mistakes. A wise one learns from others." We share these stories in the knowledge that it's simply not possible to learn entirely from the mistakes of others, and every person must endure rites of passage to make decisions that do not turn out well—sometimes repeatedly. However, we hope they offer some inspiration and will serve as cautionary tales to help you avoid similar mistakes in the same vein.

To Err is Human

Compliance is more art than science. People are unpredictable. They do dumb things, often for dumb reasons. There are multiple shades of gray.

In 2008, I was on the other end of a compliance violation. As in, I committed one. I was volunteering on a local political campaign, and I sent an internal campaign email to a journalist in order to avoid a negative media story on the party leader. In doing so, I believed I was somehow helping the party leader. In reality, my actions not only harmed the local candidate's campaign, but also violated lawyer confidentiality rules.

You see, even though I was not acting "as a lawyer" on the political campaign, I was nevertheless a lawyer. To a lay person, these might appear interchangeable. The local candidate considered me his lawyer, since he did not understand the distinction between "acting as lawyer" and "being a lawyer while engaging in other work."

I forwarded that email without a thought, in the heat of the moment. I never considered the real consequences of my actions.

The journalist ended up using that email in a negative article on the local candidate, which may have contributed to his subsequent loss in the election.

I paid dearly for that transgression. I was sued, and I was sanctioned by the Bar. It was the most intensely sad, stressful, and devastating time of my life. Once through the process, I wondered whether I could ever again serve as a chief compliance officer. Can you be a CCO if you have a track record of noncompliance? Well, fortunately, my clients thought so, and they suspected (correctly, as it turns out) that my personal integrity remained intact and that the experience would actually make me better at the job than I was before.

It made me slow down, be more thoughtful, and be more apt to consider not only what an individual may have done, but also why they may have done it. I am more objective and less judgmental. I weigh context and circumstances much more carefully now than I did before.

This assessment doesn't necessarily change the outcome of a compliance investigation, but it often changes my approach. It has given me more "humanity;" a kinder, gentler face; and the ability to connect with people in a way that breaks down hostility and combativeness and encourages constructive dialogue and reconciliation—skills that benefit us greatly in our compliance roles.

This was a hard lesson to learn. Very few readers will experience something like this. But hopefully this can serve as a reminder that the work we do as compliance officers goes beyond the strict reading of the law or policy to dictate the rules from on high.

We are human beings, and we work in companies that are made up of human beings. And while right is still right and wrong is still wrong, mistakes are inevitably made. We all need to take a moment to think carefully, consider the big picture, show compassion, and remember the weight of the position we hold and the impact we have on others.

Kristine Robidoux
QC, Senior Compliance & Regulatory Counsel
Calgary, Alberta, Canada

"

You can't control other people's actions, but you can control your reactions. This advice, also known as "control the controllables," is one I have found myself struggling to remember at times. While I can exert control over my own mindset and efforts, there is no control over the (in)actions or attitudes of others. To me, this is so profound. It helps me remember to approach all of my work with a nonjudgmental attitude. I seek to understand, and then provide perspective. It may not change the actions of others, but it allows me to know I gave my best and that I made decisions in alignment with my values and expectations and without getting emotionally entangled or frustrated.

Lisa Beth Lentini Walker
CEO
Hopkins, Minnesota

Letting Go of Her Inner Subject Matter Expert

Several years ago, when I had the chance to transition from outside health care regulatory counsel to chief compliance officer for one of my long-term clients, it seemed like a no-brainer. Who wouldn't want to step out of the world of billable hours, credit battles, and nonstop marketing required to be successful in Big Law and step into a senior executive role at a Fortune 500 company?

After representing the company for fourteen years in a broad range of regulatory, compliance, and investigation matters, I figured the learning curve would be quick and gentle. I didn't expect big changes in my day-to-day; I'd be drawing on health care legal and regulatory expertise developed over the previous fifteen years to guide and protect the company and solve problems. I knew myself well enough to know that I get a real charge out of adding value, and I believed this new role on the inside would give me even more opportunities to add value as a subject matter expert.

Of course, it wouldn't be a good Great Women in Compliance story if there weren't a lesson learned the hard way. And, for me, that lesson was that the qualities that make a successful outside lawyer or adviser are different from—and, in some ways, in conflict with—the most important quality required to succeed as a chief compliance officer: leadership.

The lesson unfolded over time. In the early days, it was just as I had expected. So many of my new colleagues welcomed me with some version of "we're so glad you are here; now we don't have to pay outside counsel rates to access your expertise." People sought out my opinion on a wide range of issues. I was able to dive into the middle of complicated problems and offer solutions. I was adding value. It felt great, and I was loving my new job.

As I was busy adding value individually, my new team was struggling. I know now that they were looking to me to set expectations and goals, to motivate and guide them, to engage them in defining a common strategy for the team. They needed a leader, not a subject matter expert.

And, in fact, the more success I had at establishing myself as the go-to compliance expert within the company, the more difficult the team dynamic became. It became clear that, for me at least, there is an inverse relationship between my ability to show up as a subject matter expert and problem solver and my ability to lead a cohesive and engaged team.

Fortunately, I had a team that gave me space to learn and grow. Part of that learning has been an intentional effort toward letting go of the drive to show up as a subject matter expert and turning it toward providing decision support to my team and empowering each team member to develop and display their subject matter expertise. When I'm successful in that effort, I can multiply the value I am able to add.

I have recently moved on to another company and another team. It's given me an opportunity to put this lesson learned to work. And, although keeping my inner subject matter expert at bay remains a challenge, the rewards of an engaged and empowered team are well worth the effort.

Lisa Estrada
Senior Vice President & Chief Compliance Officer
Nashville, Tennessee

Mind Your Mental Hygiene

Mental health and self-care is so important, but so rarely discussed in the legal industry and those careers adjacent to law, such as compliance. Your mental health is critical to everything in your personal life and your work life. Often, work culture directly impacts your mental health—and not for the better. The common view seems to be that your self-care can single-handedly address mental health stress. I don't buy this. Some work cultures cause burnout and others contribute to mental health stress due to a toxic culture or general indifference to the impact work culture can have on people.

I always knew that I should take vacations and exercise, and I was reasonably successful at doing those. Before I had kids, I would take two three- or four-week vacations at a time so that I could travel. But once I had kids, I ignored self-care; there just were not enough hours in the day or week. Or so I thought.

And until very recently, I also mistakenly thought self-care just meant luxury indulgences, like pedicures or spa days—things that do not really speak to me. I paid the price by going through a burnout. I did not take time off from work, as I knew that doing so would stress me out even further. The recovery took much longer than I expected, and I try not to lose the wisdom I gained by going through it.

But it did result in a lot of conversations in my house about what changes I needed to make and what changes we needed to make in our household as a whole. Unfortunately, it was not a conversation that took place in the workplace.

Please take care of yourself and be your own guide on what self-care means to you. Maybe it's walks in nature, painting, writing, volunteering with animals, working on a political campaign, streaming your favorite movies, exercise, reading novels, turning off your email in the evenings, saying "no" to travel that occurs over weekends, etc.

Burnout is real, and it can take a long time to recover from. I have heard from other lawyers that once you have experienced burnout, you may be easily susceptible to subsequent burnouts.

Also, please ensure that you are not contributing to burnout among your team. Are you asking for unnecessary timelines? Is your lack of planning causing you to rush others? Do you agree to unreasonable deadlines from your senior management team on behalf of your employees? Do you have a "face time" policy in your workplace, or do you take a flexible approach and allow your team to govern their schedules and come and leave from work as they may need in order to take care of their health or families? Do you have updated work-from-home policies that benefit your employees? Do you lead by example and take time away from the office as you need?

Looking back, I see that I contributed to putting unnecessary stress on people for deadlines that could have been more flexible, or for which I should have planned better. It was not fair that I may have caused them stress or took them away from tasks or work that was more important to them, or took time away from them that they could have spent doing self-care or spending with their family or friends.

Amee Sandhu
CEO, Founder & Principal Lawyer
Toronto, Ontario, Canada

"

Earlier in my career, I was always afraid of making mistakes. In retrospect, I am certain there were times I was overly concerned about getting things wrong and getting bad feedback, which kept me from forging ahead and having confidence in my work.

Later on in my career, one of the leaders I respected most talked about giving team members the freedom to fail, which would encourage creative thinking, willingness to pursue new ideas, and openness to taking some risks. A light bulb went off for me: I could make a mistake, and my boss knew that was a possibility. That statement was empowering on two levels: It was a recognition that (1) mistakes are a part of a process, and not an end, and (2) that even when I make mistakes, I am still able to be successful.

As a manager, I have taken this advice to heart, adding to it that it is important to give people the opportunity to make mistakes and that even if there is an error or a problem, I am not putting them in the position to make a mistake that we can't recover from. Now, I am able to provide comfort to anyone still concerned about the consequence of their mistakes.

I am so appreciative of the leaders who gave me the freedom to make decisions and learn from my mistakes. It has given me confidence as my career has evolved.

Lisa Fine
Director of Compliance
Washington, D.C.

38

I Know You Are, But What Am I?

It's a funny thing about ethics: We look at ourselves in the mirror, and we see a very ethical person. Heck, for some of us, we even have ethics in our titles. We look around, however, and it is easy for us to see others who just are not as ethical as we are.

We admit that we are not always honest, that we cheat a little, lie a little, maybe even steal a little. But never as much as the next person. In his book *The Honest Truth About Dishonesty: How We Lie to Everyone—Especially Ourselves*, Dan Ariely calls this the "fudge factor." We all rationalize our dishonest acts to some degree by convincing ourselves that we are not as unethical as others.

It was this very point that I was trying to illustrate to a team of vice presidents and C-Suite leaders when I got voted off the island.

This leadership team met once a month, and I had suggested to the CEO that we open each meeting with an "Integrity Minute." The concept was very much like DuPont's practice of beginning every meeting with "safety first" opener—just a short reminder about ethics to increase awareness and foster an ethical culture.

The first few Integrity Minutes went well. There were some polls about the code of conduct and sharing of metrics regarding ethics questions and concerns. Then, I conducted a short exercise called "Common Ethics" on how we perceive how ethical we are compared to others.

It went like this: Everyone had a worksheet with 10 questions. They were asked if they agreed or disagreed, if they thought their colleagues would agree or disagree, and to record the difference, recording 10% for each question where there was a difference. Then, through a show of hands, I asked how many of these leaders had recorded a difference of 100 to 80%. It was half the room. Same for the 80 to 60% range. No one had recorded a difference of less than 40%.

As this sunk in, a look of shock spread through the room. Then they were angry, realizing their colleagues did not consider them to be as ethical as they thought themselves to be.

The point was not to embarrass these leaders, but to show that we all have biases, including what Ann E. Tenbrunsel and Max H. Bazerman coined "ethical blind spots" in their book, *Blind Spots: Why We Fail to Do What's Right and What to Do About It.*

Leaders—especially those who make major decisions for their organizations—need to be aware both that they are more likely to see their own decisions as ethical (as are we all), and that others are likely to label the same decisions as unethical.

To say the message was not well-received is an understatement. My lesson learned is that while no one likes to think of themselves as unethical, leaders in particular dislike it.

Ellen M. Hunt
SVP—Audit, Ethics & Compliance Officer
Chicago, Illinois

"

Better is perfect. Things don't have to be perfect to be wonderful. I heard this for the first time from a dear friend who had been a long-time sufferer from perfectionism—so much so that at times it became debilitating to progress. Especially in our profession, with all of the pressures to have exactitude and no "failures," we all tend to focus on operating the perfect program. This advice works in all kinds of situations, including transitions, life events, and setbacks. I always try to remember that a (insert your situation) doesn't have to be perfect to be wonderful.

Lisa Beth Lentini Walker
CEO
Hopkins, Minnesota

"

Not Everyone Has the Same Definition of Ethics

I was delivering my very first ethics presentation to a group of 50 CEOs when I asked this simple question: What is one word that defines ethics for you, and would your team have the same definition? For me, this is a simple answer: Ethics means trust.

I was shocked to hear that many of these CEOs hadn't even thought about what ethics means for themselves, let alone their teams. Twelve of them stood in a line after my presentation to tell me they did not know the answer to this question and that they were going back to their offices to inquire.

The lesson I learned was that not all people have the same definition we do and that we need more clarity in our definitions. In fact, it's nearly impossible to have the same definitions unless we all have the exact same background, experience, culture, responsibilities, and religious beliefs. Doing "the right thing" means something different to each of us, and doing the right thing will lead to different outcomes depending on our definitions. If you want better outcomes, provide clearer definitions.

Another lesson I learned: It is OK to get curious. Every business issue has at its core a broken ethics value, such as lack of respect, lack of accountability, or lack of trust. If you're in the middle of an ethical dilemma, ask everyone involved to define ethics and the ethical thing to do, and watch what unfolds. It should definitely reframe the challenge you're facing and lead to clearer communication, and it might even direct you to the root cause of the issue you're trying to resolve.

Marcy Maslov
Chief Integrity Builder
Phoenix, Arizona

Chapter Four

Diversity Matters

Lisa says...

" Many of us remember that old stereotype of a board-room: a bunch of older white men sitting at a table wearing loosened ties as if they were "in action." That's where we start the discussion of who has a seat at the table.

I never wanted to be at that table in an office or in life, but I did want to lead and bring my voice and the voices of others to make sure there was representation. It is a constant challenge, but a critically important one.

The Great Women in Compliance Podcast started as #MeToo came to the forefront, and with the Black Lives Matter movement in 2020, we have yet another opportunity to reflect on diversity and how we can all make an impact.

Compliance professionals have the unique opportunity to shape an organization's ethical culture in the job by promoting a diverse workforce. This can not only lead to more opportunities for individuals who may not have had opportunities in the past—both in joining organizations and succeeding—but also ensure that all risks and viewpoints are heard. As **Fabiana Lacerca-Allen** notes below, if you do not do this, you will not have all of the best minds at the table.

Similarly, compliance professionals have a great opportunity to make our professional community more diverse. By doing so, we can help build networks and communities to remove barriers for talented newcomers and make sure they are equipped with the tools for continued success in ethics and compliance.

And, as Mary said at the beginning of Chapter 1, we value fairness, justice, and doing the right thing. Making diversity a priority is one way to do this, just as the women describe in these stories.

,,

Build a Diverse Bench

I often mentor women who are super accomplished, bright, and eager to prove themselves. While they have everything necessary to have a great career in corporate America, they often are worrying about the wrong thing or don't know their true worth in the workplace.

So many times, women worry about how people view them, or they put a lot of focus on being "nice." While it is crucial to be empathetic and kind to others, women fret about how their peers perceive them; their male counterparts usually do not have the same worries.

44

Women have a duty to fight for themselves and each other. You truly do not succeed unless you bring up others with you. And you do not have the best minds around the table if you are not looking at a diverse group of people.

Fabiana Lacerca-Allen
SVP & CCO
Hayward, California

"

Don't let someone dictate what you should be doing for a living because of their preconceived idea based on how you look or sound.

When I moved to the U.S., several seasoned professionals tried to dissuade me from being a business lawyer and a compliance professional, saying I should work with immigration law (because I speak a few different languages). I heard their advice, thanked them, and continued to move toward my goal.

For me, the key is doing it with grace so you never burn bridges (or are perceived as burning bridges). It's important to build resilience along the way, because you won't hear it just a couple of times…

Fernanda Beraldi
Senior Director, Ethics & Compliance
Indianapolis, Indiana

Nurture the Conversation

Because diversity matters, our voices matter. In my workplace, I use my voice to have open discussions about areas of improvement, plans for improvement, and how we will monitor progress.

As the ethics and compliance leader, I have led trainings on how to have open conversations—not confrontations—on uncomfortable subjects like Black Lives Matter, diversity, equity and inclusion, unconscious bias, and ethical leadership. I show how women and minorities' experiences are intrinsically intertwined in each of those topics.

The first step in fixing a problem is knowing there is a problem in the first place. I believe that in order to improve women and minority representation and experiences, changes in behavior must be coupled with changes in accountability. Thus, just like we do in compliance, we have to test and monitor how effective the plans we put in place actually are—and hold departments accountable for not complying.

Asha Palmer
Chief Ethics & Compliance Officer
Montclair, New Jersey

"

I started my career in Compliance in 2011, and I made a vow back then that no matter how high I go, I will always give back. I started mentoring at every stage of my career. Whether serving as compliance auditor or director of compliance audit, I always made time to mentor and open doors for others.

As an African American woman in health care compliance, I did not see many other African American women in compliance leadership roles, and I decided that I wanted to change that as well. I made it a point to educate and engage young African American women by speaking at local high school career fairs and mentoring young women of color through organizations like Big Brothers Big Sisters. Many of these young women were not even aware that health care compliance existed. Because of those efforts, 20 of the women I have mentored are now in compliance or coding roles in their organizations.

My favorite Bible verse: "To whom much is given, much is required." Meaning in order for me to truly be great, I cannot forget to send the elevator back down.

Leslie Boles
Director of Compliance Audit
Dallas, Texas

"

Extend a Hand

In the midst of the COVID-19 pandemic, we have seen civil unrest that demands we all re-examine how we treat each other in our society, workplaces, schools, and even in our homes. As **Ellen Hunt** notes, we also lost a number of civil rights icons, including Congressman John Lewis, who coined the term "good trouble" to describe nonviolent protest of racial inequality.

Getting into good trouble has a long history—from Susan B. Anthony, who fought for women's right to vote, to Martin Luther King, Jr., who championed for equal rights, and now to every ethics and compliance professional who should be the conscience of the organization, just as John Lewis was the conscience of Congress. Lewis asked all to "answer the highest calling of your heart" and stand up for what you truly believe, and he encouraged all of us to "stand up, speak up, and speak out." To be able to do this, we need to reach out.

I have often remarked that, as wonderful as it is to be with other ethics and compliance professionals, we spend too much time together. We all like and are most comfortable with people who speak the same language, have similar backgrounds, and do what we do. But this is not how we can serve an organization as its conscience.

In sponsoring and mentoring others, I encourage ethics and compliance folks to get to know the auditors, the risk management staff, the people who report to the chief financial officer … actually anyone at all who does something other than ethics and compliance. It may not be what many consider encouraging diversity or fighting against racial inequality in the traditional sense, but I think it's critical for those who want to have a culture that fosters ethical behavior and compliance with the law.

So, this is my small way of encouraging diversity and introducing others to what ethics and compliance is all about. This is how I raise some good trouble:

- Seek out others who are not in ethics and compliance.

- Never say "no" to an opportunity to speak, write, or present; instead, give it to someone who might not otherwise have the chance.

- Look for and give opportunities to others.

- Always make time for someone who asks for help—any kind of help.

- Sponsor and mentor anyone.

- Listen carefully to what your colleagues are concerned about and figure out how to make it better.

- Actively support others in achieving their goals, both professional and personal.

- Challenge the status quo—specifically outdated rules.

Won't you please join me?

Ellen M. Hunt
SVP—Audit, Ethics & Compliance Officer
Chicago, Illinois

Reaching Out to Encourage Speaking Up

I have been a dedicated compliance professional for more than sixteen years in the manufacturing industry. I've always believed and promoted the principle that everyone matters and, more importantly, what we do as individuals and teams matters.

I have made it my practice to tour every location I visit so I can interact individually with hourly production employees and gain a better understanding of the environment in which they work daily. This helps build trust, encourages reporting, and helps develop dialogue that encourages us to respect and celebrate our differences. In my visits to manufacturing locations, I came to realize that hourly production employees' contributions and concerns are often overlooked. This is where we find higher cross-populations of minorities.

My focus is not only on the hourly production employees, but it's an important segment of our workforce. My goal is to support and promote diversity so that all employees feel welcomed, included, valued, supported, and able to succeed. This begins with creating an environment that invites dialogue.

Cindy Morrison
Director of Compliance
St. Louis, Missouri

"

In this period of renewed effort to dismantle the social and structural impediments that have contributed to racial disparities in every aspect of American life, as an African American compliance professional, I couldn't help thinking about the special role risk and compliance professionals play in advancing social change, particularly in corporate settings.

As risk and compliance officers, we are often the gatekeepers and managers of risk—in all of its forms. And we know from repeated experience that the absence of diversity and inclusion in decision-making creates inevitable blind spots and leads to unmitigated organizational risk.

Given this recurring observation, it is my sincere belief that, beyond its intangible benefits, diversity and inclusion are integral to effective risk governance. I believe that, given our rapidly changing demographics, organizations that grasp this concept early will experience better risk outcomes and a more sustained competitive advantage.

Jennifer D. Newton
Founder & CEO
Miami, Florida

Opening Doors by Banning Bias

The most meaningful approach I can offer when it comes to gender and racial equity in the workplace is based on my own reflection and experience. Many years ago, while working at a large enterprise, two amazing female corporate leaders and attorneys gave me the opportunity to start an ethics and compliance function. While I had the skill set to take the discipline and role on, I didn't fit the legal compliance profile, not having come from private practice.

These two women saw past what was on paper and got to know me. They assessed my knowledge, saw my drive, and appreciated the perspective I was bringing to the global role as a woman of color. They not only opened the door, they went a step further, both mentoring me. Their mentorship served to enhance those legal skills and experience that some might consider lacking on paper.

Based on this reflection, here is my approach to increasing women and minorities in the compliance and ethics space:

Expand what you think you know about compliance and ethics roles and what you think is "required" experience. Consider what a diverse person might know, their alignment to a role according to knowledge, and their skill, perspective, and confidence. Be conscious of the bias that will creep in if someone doesn't meet the conventional CV outline you've seen a million times. Be careful not to outright exclude a woman or minority in a discipline that is otherwise heavily represented by a "majority" class.

Talk to leaders about their hiring practices. Talk openly. There's no better time to engage, and there are so many resources available to support engaging all colleagues about the focus on gender and racial equality. It's time to be brave. You won't regret it.

Give back. I never stop looking around and responding to opportunities to lift a female or diverse person up. Seize a moment that could make a difference in someone being promoted, being extended an offer, or being accepted to a program or school. Those two leaders gave back to me as I began my compliance career, so I do the same: I give back with whatever means I have to lift someone up from an underrepresented class or community. Without being asked.

Monica Lopez Reinmiller
Ethics, Risk & Compliance Professional
Bellevue, Washington

A Silent Volcano and a Push for Inclusion

In the midst of a global pandemic and very unprecedented times, the events of May 25, 2020, sent the world into further unrest and bring to the surface another deep-rooted epidemic.

But why now? Why is the Black Lives Matter movement different from all the others? Why does it have a global application, resulting in a global movement? What does it mean for the industry, how does it impact the firm, and what should we be doing or not doing?

These were all questions asked simultaneously by firms in a desperate rush to garner understanding and insight for acting "safely!"

Two of my overarching responses:

It was almost like a silent volcano waiting to explode. It was the compounding effect of a series of recent events which seemed to be ongoing, and the disproportionate adverse impact of COVID. The Black community globally got tired, fed up, and vulnerable. It was very easy to join the historical dots globally and achieve a translation across the various geographical regions, birthing Black Lives Matter!

Quite rightly, education is a significant component and a starting point to address the problem, but it can't be the sole approach. This isn't an academic study or science, and it can't be resolved as such. There needs to be a willingness to be in "unsafe territory," to be comfortable being very uncomfortable, to be vulnerable, to listen, to challenge oneself and one's inner biases, to broaden the scope of integrity beyond the professional lens.

Initial education and insight have been delivered in multiple formats and will continue, causing pause, reflection, and a reality check. This is needed to progress the conversation. But how do we move the dial from reflection to change?

A couple of considerations:

The flood of guilt and empathy has been encouraging, but it isn't a strategy, and firms can't stop there.

This has to be treated in a way not to cause further divide or fatigue.

Each individual, department, and firm are at different points in their journeys, hence actions will vary depending on where along the journey they are!

In solving for the most sensitive and problematic diversity strand, firms can become truly inclusive and not just diverse!

Sisieta Owen
Global Head of Regulatory Compliance,
Monitoring & Testing Pillar
London, United Kingdom

Lessons from a
Post-Apartheid South Africa

Diversity in the demographic profile of an organization or team matters—a great deal. It matters in ways that make a significant difference to the performance and sustainability of a business and to the experience of those who work in and are served by it.

Credible studies have linked diversity in team composition to, amongst others benefits, increased innovation and enhanced decision-making. This is not surprising; in groups of like-minded people with overly similar life experiences and perspectives, debate is inherently limited and output naturally compromised.

Beyond the significant performance and profitability benefits of diversity in the workplace, the absence of diversity in a country's organizations represents a failure to achieve a state of socioeconomic justice.

There is a single question to ask when assessing the status quo and identifying the desired future state of an organization's level of diversity: To what extent does the existing demographic profile of the workforce match that of the economically active population? Having a clear understanding of the gap between these two sets of data—specifically with regard to race and gender at every level of the organization—positions us to develop and implement strategies to move toward a more ideal future state.

My earliest career experience of having to embrace seemingly incompatible objectives and yet pursue them all—simultaneously and successfully—was when I led a major workforce diversity transformation. The board's mandate was clear: improve performance across the business, expand services, reduce costs (including headcount), and increase the extent to which the employee complement matches the demographic profile of the country's population of economically active people.

It was South Africa in the early 1990s, and companies were preparing for a post-apartheid era in which global competitiveness would replace isolationist economic policies and in which active redress would need to be taken to overcome the injustices of the past, when so many had been denied the opportunity of studying or working in areas of their choosing.

The lessons gleaned from the decades of transformation that followed would take a dedicated volume to share. With the benefit of hindsight and having observed comparative successes and failures across different South African organizations, these are a few of the insights that I especially wish to share with those willing or required to increase organizational diversity:

Sustainable change is achieved slowly. Underestimating the need to prepare and manage the organizational culture for a change in the demographic profile will make new appointments short-lived and early progress easily undone.

Play the long game. Attracting candidates with a view to increasing diversity by offering remuneration premiums may help you meet short-term diversity goals, but unless the work environment offers a holistic match between what's sought by and then experienced by the new entrant, the appointment will not succeed in the medium term. Such candidates are vulnerable to other premium offers, and the differential you pay can destroy the fairness experienced by your existing employees.

Identifying and removing barriers to entry by underrepresented group members must be an overriding priority. From within the organization, it is easy to be unaware of existing barriers, be they inadvertently created or otherwise. Understanding the experiences and perspectives of existing employees from underrepresented groups is a valuable step toward identifying and devising ways to overcome both real and perceived barriers.

For sustainable progress, focus on recruitment. Progress toward both the performance and transformation goals of an organization requires significant attention to recruitment, and specifically to sourcing a pool of candidates that includes strong applicants from the underrepresented groups. It must become a priority to dedicate enough time to finding such candidates, tempering our preoccupation with placement speed. Having attracted diverse and capable applicants, appointments can be made on merit and the organization can avoid the perception that a candidate's success was determined by race or gender.

Be ever vigilant for prejudice in the selection process. We are all prone to the adverse influence of stereotypes on what we think is an objective assessment of candidates. Owning the fact that we may be subjective in our response to a candidate is an essential precursor to making objective decisions.

Incorporate objective measures into the selection process. Data that unequivocally demonstrates a candidate's superior performance on standardized measures may be the only basis on which a doggedly diversity-averse line manager will shift from preferring the candidate that is their closest demographic match.

Position each new appointment on the grounds of suitability and competence. Take care to not inadvertently brand the new entrant as a "diversity appointment." This is essential for the dignity, respect, and cooperation experienced by and accorded to the new team member.

Avoid alienating existing employees from overrepresented groups. These are experienced and mostly valuable members who deserve to feel confident their future is secure, provided they are willing to play a constructive role in ensuring the success and sustainability of the organization's diversity program.

Don't overlook the importance of increasing diversity at lower levels of the organization. In the long-term, the progress you make today at the entry and middle levels will ensure that in the future, the organization's makeup at all levels is an accurate reflection of the demographic profile of your country.

Penny Milner-Smyth
Organizational Behavior, Workplace Ethics &
Anti-Corruption Compliance Specialist
Durban, KwaZulu-Natal, South Africa

Chapter Five

Well THAT Was Embarrassing

Mary says...

" No matter how prepared you are, no matter how classy you are in your best moments, there are sudden potholes in the journey of life that are truly and utterly mortifying. Some of these moments occur in our work capacity, which somehow makes them even more egregiously humiliating. We are expected to be perfectly polished. Professional. But we humans are fallible; at times, less-than-ideal circumstances befall us, and the veil of professionalism gives way.

I say "veil" because no one is constantly thinking of how to be professional in their home life. It's something we put on for the workplace, much like my favorite peplum dress for giving presentations. So why is it that we feel so awful when something we apply strictly for business purposes is pulled away a little?

I have come to accept that, in the moment, it can feel like the world has ended, yet the silver lining of embarrassing mishaps in the workplace is plentiful, especially for compliance officers.

To reframe the situation, it's a real opportunity to prove just how human and relatable you are. As **Rebecca Walker** shares in this chapter, in those moments, the opportunity is ripe to find the humor, establish common ground, and build rapport with your stakeholders.

So, while I will not wish you any more embarrassing moments than life is currently throwing at you, I invite you to see the opportunities those moments present to connect with your audience in a less conventional way. **"**

The Compliance Lady with the Weak American Stomach

I was working for a company that had recently opened its first-ever location in pretty much the middle of nowhere India. It was a four-hour, winding, hairpin-curve drive over the mountains from the nearest international airport, and then another hour past the nearest city of any size. I was visiting to provide an introduction to the compliance program and implement a "train the trainer" model to empower local management to build their own culture of compliance.

I had been warned by other employees who had worked on the initial opening of the facility that I should not eat at the local employee cafeteria or restaurants and, instead, bring my own food from home and only drink bottled water, lest I get sick. I was sternly advised not to eat anything that hadn't been boiled or peeled.

I carefully loaded my suitcase with protein bars, crackers, nuts, beef jerky, bottled water, all the basics. I was at the local facility for a little over a week and carefully avoided eating really anything that I hadn't brought with me except for maybe a banana or two. By the end of the week, I was down to my last sleeve of crackers, which I ate for breakfast, and was quite proud of myself as I had successfully avoided any intestinal issues during my stay.

Unbeknownst to me, however, the local management team had planned an elaborate "thank you" lunch in my honor, given it was my last day there. They had ordered in multiple local dishes for me to try. I had no idea what to do. They seated me at a place of honor with all of the local management team and promptly escorted me to the head of the buffet line so I could have first choice of all the entrees. All eyes were on me as fifty people or so waited behind for me to serve myself first.

What could I do? I felt like it would be the epitome of rudeness to refuse to eat anything, given that the lunch was literally thrown in my honor. I thought to myself, "Well, rice is cooked in boiling water, right? It is probably safe to eat. And the curry was probably cooking all day, so I'm sure anything that might have been in there has been cooked out at this point. I'll try a little of that too. I'm sure it's fine."

So, I gingerly helped myself to small portions of rice and some chicken, which I nibbled at politely, but avoided eating too much of. When lunch was over, I thanked everyone and climbed into the van for the five-hour trip back through town and over the hairpin-curve mountain roads to the airport for my evening flight home. I only made it about halfway through the drive before I started getting sick. We had to pull over multiple times for me to retch on the side of the road. I barely made it back in time for my flight, which turned out to be the longest flight of my life.

My driver was a local facility employee who promptly called the local management team to tell them I was sick. They in turn called the company doctor, who notified our local corporate security team, who sent someone to meet me at the airport to ensure I was OK. Suffice it to say, word traveled fast, and from that point on, I was known locally as the "compliance lady with the weak American stomach." For years, whenever I spoke or emailed with people from that facility they would always ask me if I was the one who got sick. So embarrassing, but ultimately, it made me very memorable!

Gwendolyn Lee Hassan
Director & Managing Counsel, Global Compliance
Oak Park, Illinois

When You Step in It...

I was in a meeting with an executive, my boss, and a senior vice president from a business unit. My boss, the SVP, and I were trying to convince the executive to let us go through our process instead of elevating an issue directly to the CEO.

I explained to him that he needed to trust our process and how we were dealing with it. At first, he didn't agree with us. He left the meeting for a couple of minutes to take an urgent phone call and, upon coming back, he said that he trusted my opinion and that we could proceed with our process. He also thanked me for having had the courage to stand up to him when the other people in the room didn't.

At the time, I remember thinking that my boss didn't say anything during the meeting to convince the executive of our process, and that given what he said to me, the executive might have not been impressed with the silence from my boss. So, I responded that we were a team and that the three of us had agreed on this approach with each other prior to meeting with him.

The executive responded by saying that I was still the only one who had the courage to stand up to him.

You know when you get a compliment but at the same time it disparages everyone else in the room, and you think, how can I shift the tension? How can I make sure we all look good?

So I said that as a minority, I didn't have any choice but to stand up for myself.

Oh my God, did I just say that?

He responded by saying, "Oh, you're playing the gender card now!"

I had to think quickly to get out of the hole I had dug. So, I answered, "It has nothing to do with gender. I'm the only one that still has hair in this room. I'm playing the follicles card!"

Everyone laughed. Humor saved the moment! From that day I earned his respect, and he always considered me as a true advisor.

Patricia Alleyn
Head of Integrity Program
Montreal, Canada

Accepting Awards with Amazing Grace

It was 2014, and I was closing out my third year as general counsel for the Americas division of a global company. I had gotten my sea legs and felt steady in the role.

Being a general counsel meant I joined the ranks of the company's global senior management team, a privilege that, as a woman of color, I did not take for granted. The "SMT," as we called it, met annually to learn from our challenges, celebrate our successes, and plan for the year ahead. Our 2014 meeting ended with an elegant dinner that included the entire SMT, the board of directors, and other guests. All in, roughly 150 people gathered in a beautiful ballroom. It was the kind of night that makes you feel a part of something truly special.

The evening included an awards ceremony to recognize accomplishments across operations and around the globe. There I sat, enjoying dinner and camaraderie with colleagues. Suddenly, I hear the CEO call my name. A strategic project on which I had worked was being recognized. I stand up proudly and walk confidently as the only woman on the team to join eight of my male colleagues. I make my way across the long stage, shaking hand after hand. If only my parents could see me now!

I take a step back ready to settle into my place alongside the all-male team ... and I feel ... absolutely nothing.

Literally. Nothing.

Time stops and I am flying ... ever so slowly ... off the stage (in three-inch heels and a cocktail dress). A collective gasp rises across the ballroom.

To this day, I have no idea how I did it—whether it was muscle memory from childhood days spent jumping off high-flying swings or the sheer will to preserve my last shred of dignity—but I did it ... I actually stuck the landing. There I was, both feet firmly planted, dress intact, and heels still on! I shoot up, throw both hands straight into the air, stare straight at the audience, and yell (in equal parts shock and celebration), "I'M OK! I'M

OK!" The room erupts into laughter and applause. I return to my seat with my award and my dignity.

Alejandra Montenegro Almonte
Vice Chair, International Department & Member
Washington, D.C.

The Stranger at Breakfast

I am fairly decent at remembering names and faces, but not if I have never encountered them before. At a conference breakfast recently, I was happily munching away on my bacon when a tall, bearded gentleman sat down next to me.

I quickly finished chewing, smiled, put my hand out, and said, "Good morning, my name is Jenny Kim. I am with Koch Industries."

He shook my hand and responded, "Good morning, I am John Smith, and I am from the state attorney general's office." (I am leaving out his name for the sake of anonymity). I nodded and continued to smile. "Great to meet you."

We started to idle on topics, such as current events, the state of criminal justice reform, and how Koch Industries was playing a role in his state's criminal justice reform efforts. He then asked me if I was really a lawyer.

I kept smiling and nodded. "Yes, I am an attorney for Koch Industries. So, what do you do for the state attorney general's office?" The tall, bearded man looked at me over his glasses, kept silent, and then lifted his napkin to wipe his lips. He then responded, "I am the State Attorney General."

My eyes widened and I forced myself to keep smiling. I awkwardly stated, "Ah, I should have known... so... what are the priorities in your AG office, and do you know about second chance hiring?"

As it turned out, this state AG strongly supported the practice and knew personally many of the companies that make these hires. We compared notes and discussed how to ensure the success of second chance hiring. He offered to introduce me to some second chance companies—and with that and an exchange of cards, our breakfast ended.

Jenny Kim
Deputy General Counsel, Political Law & VP,
Public Policy
Washington, D.C.

"

Use humor when you can. While I'm not naturally a funny person (I bought a book in law school called *How to be Funny*, which was not particularly effective), I am a true believer in the ability of humor to get through sticky situations.

When I first started my compliance law practice, I worked from home. I had carefully instructed my then three-year-old (now nineteen-year-old!) daughter not to answer my work phone. Of course, inevitably, Emma answered the phone when the in-house lawyer of my most important client called. ("Hewo. Who this?") My face turned red (it always does), and I grabbed the phone from her chubby little fingers and said "Hi, Gary. I'm so glad you got the chance to meet my assistant." He laughed, regaled me with tales of his own three-year-old, and we got past it. When you're embarrassed, look for the opportunity to lighten the mood with humor.

Rebecca Walker
Compliance Lawyer
Santa Monica, California

When You Know, Go.

One of the best forms of self-care is to go where you are celebrated—not merely tolerated. I believe it was author and motivational speaker Paul F. Davis who originally said this. It is so true, especially for women or minority groups who already face so many additional obstacles.

Otherwise, you will be diverting emotional energy to bolster yourself in order to just survive your environment. And it may not be so bad initially. You may not realize this is even happening. But over time, it can have a corrosive effect on you, your relationships at work, your productivity, the quality of your work, and worse, your relationships with your dear ones at home.

The difference is like sailing with the wind to your back, versus sailing into the wind. You may still get to your destination, but you may arrive much later than planned, exhausted, and without having enjoyed the scenery.

You are worth it. You are a tremendous person and professional. If your manager, team, corporate culture, etc., don't treat you that way, don't stay where you are. This may mean looking for other options internally, leaving the organization, or if those are not options, finding communities outside of the workforce that support you in this way. Otherwise, it's too easy to doubt yourself.

If you feel it's time to leave an organization or that over time, things have changed and you are not getting the support you used to have (or should have), trust your instincts. If it's time to leave, it's time to leave. It can be hard to recognize this in a timely way.

Amee Sandhu

Practice Patience

Sometimes you have to let things run their course, which can take time. (This is ironic coming from me, since I am likely to be the least patient person in any room.)

Here's my angle: in virtually every organization—especially the large ones—there are people with a mediocre work ethic, unimpressive knowledge, and terrible people skills who somehow skate by—or are even rewarded. Some of them know other people in high places, particularly if they are of a privileged gender and/or race. Some of them take credit for others' ideas, pass the buck, and refuse to assume responsibility when things go wrong, even when it's on their watch. They may be in leadership positions, but they are assuredly not leaders. And they may make your life miserable at work. So, why am I advocating patience in the face of these unfortunate and unfair facts? Because, believe it or not, these charlatans are almost always found out—and their day almost always comes.

How do I know that? Well, I once had a job that I enjoyed at a company that I loved. Then a friend of a board member was installed in a senior leadership position he had no business being in. And he made my life—and many others' lives—miserable. He tried to get me fired on more than one occasion. Many people left because of him. I almost quit more than once.

Then my father shared this very same advice with me. He said people like this are eventually exposed and then let go. He told me that the process always takes far too long, and he suggested that, if I liked my job and didn't want to leave, I should ride it out for a bit longer. He was right. I lasted, but that member of senior management did not.

Andrea Falcione

Chapter Six

Productivity Hacks

Tips from the Trenches

Mary says...

" I'm not sure if it's because I fall into the millennial category (stereotypically known for being impatient), but I'm a big fan of getting stuff done and not having to reinvent the wheel, as **Amee Sandhu** so aptly describes one of my bugbears below. For this reason, I was keen to include a knowledge-sharing section in the book to help Great Women in Compliance be even more efficient and effective in their jobs. When we help each other out, all of our boats rise.

We fall into a unique category in compliance where speaking with other compliance counterparts at other companies, even competitors, about many aspects of the compliance program is unlikely to trigger antitrust risk. We can make the most of this by sharing our best practices, our time saving tips, our templates, and our collective knowledge.

For example, I find it incredibly useful to employ the voice messenger features of iMessage, Whatsapp, Facebook Messenger, and even LinkedIn to communicate with team members when in a hurry. This is particularly so when traveling and it's not possible to pull out my laptop and draft a lengthy message by touch typing—it's very efficient for sending complex messages for work or to add a personal touch.

With Whatsapp, I can even record these messages while flying and without access to Wi-Fi, queue them up to send, and they'll automatically be sent once I'm wheels down and have connectivity again.

I consider traveling to be "dead time," so quickly delegating some tasks before take-off is an easy way to stay productive and avoid a long to-do list after disembarking from a lengthy flight. You do have to take into account any security issues, of course, so be careful with the exact content you're sharing across these lines of communication, and ensure you're complying with your internal data security policies.

Want more tips? You've come to the right place. This chapter covers both hard skills and soft—from **Ola Tucker**'s step-by-step guide for training success to **Beth Colling**'s formula to make networking easy, we've got you covered.

If you identify a key takeaway from this chapter that you start implementing to make your life easier right away, don't forget to keep the knowledge circulating and share the tip with another Great Woman in Compliance.

Tell someone you know or reach a wider audience by sharing on social media. Social media sharing is one of the best routes to efficiently disseminate valuable information, build your personal brand, and display subject matter expertise and thought leadership all at once. How productive is that?!

An Accessible Approach to Networking

While I inherently know that establishing work relationships is important, the concept of "networking" once seemed an exhausting waste of time. Networking is reserved for salespeople and politicians. I had no plans to go into either profession, so why bother?

But in 2013, I attended a program at the Harvard Kennedy School led by Stacy Blake-Beard, a Professor of Management at the Simmons School of Business in Boston. One of her areas of expertise is teaching women the importance of building networks.

In taking this class, I made a list of people I know in three ways: those to whom I have a close connection (people I see daily), those to whom I have a moderate connection (people I see every once in a while), and those whom I see only once or twice a year. That list looked exhausting to me. I didn't have enough time in my day to complete my work and see my family, much less "network."

But it turns out that there is actually merit in connecting to people in a meaningful way. I learned that I should focus on only two of the three lists. The moderate connections (the people we see only every once in a while) are usually never the ones you trust, so eliminate that list. From the other two lists, focus on three to five people in each. Then make a commitment to reach out to one person in each list just once a week.

Blake-Beard recommends keeping a journal specifically for this and providing reminders to yourself. This was networking in an organized fashion that I could actually understand!

In the end, I found a group of people who became my sounding board, mentors, and gurus of life. I just wish I had started sooner.

M. Beth Colling
Senior Vice President & Chief Compliance Officer
Boston, Massachusetts

Ola Tucker's Top Training Tips

- Engage employees by asking them to share stories of compliance-related issues they've encountered and how they resolved them.

- Ask a member of senior management to highlight a specific instance where an employee successfully navigated a compliance-related issue. This can be done at staff meetings or via email. Be sure to describe the specific compliance issue encountered and how it was addressed.

- Use a recent news story, scandal, or enforcement action to point out a specific compliance violation and its resulting consequences. Then highlight the specific policies and procedures your company has in place to address such situations.

- Share short video clips from popular films and television shows to help explain compliance-related concepts, such as money laundering, securities violations, or cybercrime. (Netflix has several series that are great for this, as well as entertaining).

- Send out a short email highlighting Top Ten Compliance-Related Facts or Figures. This should be something that grabs the reader's attention and can be read in a minute or less.

- Email a list of compliance-related FAQs with links to applicable compliance policies.

- Maintain an updated compliance page on your company's intranet site and notify employees when there are significant updates to the site.

- Create compliance-related infographics on specific compliance risks or topics, such as third-party risk or suspicious activity red flags.

- Host a companywide contest where employees submit a compliance-related infographic for a modest prize, such as a gift card.

- Recognize and celebrate compliance-themed days, such as Data Privacy Day or International Anti-Corruption Day. Use these as specific opportunities to raise awareness and promote best practices throughout the company.

Ola Tucker
Compliance Writer & Training Consultant
Wilmington, Delaware

Go to the Source

The "seven elements of an effective compliance program" have been with us since the dawn of compliance. As a quick review, these seven elements derive from two sources: the *U.S. Sentencing Guidelines on Effective Compliance Programs*, often referred to by compliance professionals as the Federal Sentencing Guidelines, and the Department of Health and Human Services Office of Inspector General's *Compliance Program Guidance* documents (there are several).

The seven elements are summaries of these much more detailed documents. Unfortunately, when something gets summarized, important details often get lost.

Productivity Hack: Read the source materials that govern your organization and align your programs with the sources, not the summaries. Design your own "seven elements"—or eight or nine or ten—to ensure all the bases get covered.

Here is how I did that:

I rearranged the seven elements to be in harmony with business process principles, and I added an eighth element: leadership and organizational culture. I did this because different leaders are given different responsibilities in the Federal Sentencing Guidelines. In addition, leaders and culture are critically important for compliance to be successful.

I often remark that without these key elements, even a perfect seven elements-based program will eventually end up in a black hole.

Leverage the source material and make it work for you.

Deena King
Chief Compliance Officer
Tyler, Texas

As I look back on my corporate career and the additional information I have been able to acquire as an advisor to small and large corporations, I want to remind our next generation of women in compliance to focus first and foremost on understanding both your company's primary business goals and strategies and the related risk issues it faces.

As a compliance professional, your ability to influence others will be successful if your management, peers, and subordinates know that your compliance efforts are geared toward assisting them accomplish their goals while still protecting the company. A compliance professional must not work in a regulatory or legal silo, so the ability to establish relationships is critical to success in this field.

One way to establish these relationships is to show that you are able to fully understand the business goals of the various functions in your organization and their accompanying risks. This will allow you to function as an enabler, and your advice and counsel will be sought out and welcomed by others in the company.

Haydee Olinger
Former Global Chief Compliance Officer
Chicago, Illinois

Build Bridges, Not Walls

Don't build walls around silos. Or between headquarters and others business units, either. Build bridges instead.

Some of my most effective initiatives have been collaborations. Often, what we do in the compliance and ethics office overlaps with responsibilities in other functions (legal, HR, risk management, audit, finance, employee communications, government relations, information governance, etc.). Even when the CEO or some other senior leader tells you that something is the responsibility of the compliance and ethics department, that's not necessarily going to smooth any ruffled feathers when other departments assume you're stepping on their remit.

Besides, we can learn from and even defer to the experience and expertise of these other functions, rather than starting from scratch.

Take for example employee surveys. Partnering with HR to do a "culture of integrity" survey can make for a much more effective launch. They've done employee surveys, and they know the channels and messaging to help make it as effective as possible. In fact, combining my culture surveys with HR's employee engagement surveys yielded a much better response rate than sending out my own culture survey.

Similarly, by choreographing our work with the audit department, compliance audits can piggyback on other audits. This is often greatly appreciated by employees who don't need to be interrupted twice for audit interviews. This is also true for risk assessments; the finance or risk management departments are likely in charge of running the enterprise risk management program, but their protocols can miss risk areas we care about in compliance and ethics.

Trying to run a separate process is a nonstarter when a much bigger, very robust process is already running routinely across the organization. Ultimately, we want the people potentially creating risks across the organization to feel responsible for managing those risks proactively. By coordinating with the ERM process, we can ensure that our risks are managed through the same processes that drive accountability in the ERM systems.

Debra Sabatini Hennelly
Consulting Firm Principal & Former
General Counsel / CCO
Neptune Township, New Jersey

Make a Plan, Work the Plan

Charlotte Young says an effective three-year compliance program starts with establishing the "Big Picture Mission." Step two is setting key objectives that you intend to reach over the next three years, followed by assigning specific actions that will help you achieve that mission.

What's next? Measuring!

"This can be the most difficult part; measuring success in our industry is the topic of much discussion and hand-wringing. Stay away from measurements of performance (such as number of people trained) in favor of measurements of engagement and learning. You may not be able to find a measurement for every course of action. You also should have measurements for every year of the three-year plan. They can increase over the three-year plan, such as 20% year one, 50% year two, etc."

Charlotte recommends spreading the action steps over a multi-year program with care, "making sure that you don't front load and that you leave some actions for later years. Think about how your program will be viewed, and ensure that the strategy is clear—and remember that mission!"

Finally, Charlotte recommends creating a high-level document to state the mission and the objectives.

"It can be used as a reporting tool—as a one-page document to show your priorities and focus—for the board, your C-suite colleagues, or even the public. Post it on your home page to show accountability. Then get to work."

Charlotte Young
Chief Risk & Compliance Officer
Arlington, Virginia

Who Do You Think You Are?

Of the five key leadership elements that get you promoted, self-awareness is number one. It is fundamental to effective leadership. In simple terms, it is the ability to be introspective, to accurately reflect on our behaviors, emotions, and attitudes. It is the foundational element of emotional intelligence, as expressed by thought leader Daniel Goleman, and it has been cited as one of the top two reasons leaders succeed or fail.

Self-awareness enables you to view yourself objectively, without judgment. And if you have an accurate and honest view of yourself, this enables you to make good decisions and quickly course-correct, if necessary.

So let's kick off with five valuable things you can do to increase your self-awareness:

1. Know Your Why, How, and What

It's important in your career (and your personal life) to be able to clearly articulate your values, motivations, and interests. When you're aware of your preferences and aversions, **you can make intentional, well-considered choices that lead to greater success and personal fulfillment.** Recently, one of my clients was given feedback that his interpersonal style was impacting his ability to inspire trust and influence others. He doesn't value interpersonal interaction per se, or need a lot of approval, so summoning the motivation to shift his interactions is a potential challenge for him.

We revisited his values and are reframing the behavior change to align with his strong preference for flawless execution and having fun at work. To start exploring this for yourself, **think about what motivates you to do your best work.** Is it the opportunity to be a technical expert, solving a problem no one else has resolved? Supporting your team emotionally through challenges like a reorganization? The feeling you get when you rally people to action? Recognize and note the moments when you are operating at your best. These reflections will help reveal your why, how, and what.

2. Understand What Sets You Off

When was the last time you lost your temper at work, beat yourself up over a mistake, or became unnecessarily competitive? **Pick one emotional reaction that is not serving you, and start noticing when this behavior is triggered.** Keep a journal for a week and note the circumstances of the event and the thoughts that come to mind. Chances are, your internal emotions are showing up externally. If you're aware, you can work to change your reaction habits.

3. Seek Out Your Blind Spots

Are you aware of the behaviors that may be decreasing your leadership effectiveness? The most effective way to comprehensively expose blind spots is to do what's called a 360 review, where work colleagues confidentially provide candid developmental feedback evaluations, which are debriefed with you by a trained coach. A quick step in this direction is for you to ask your boss, "What one thing could I do to be more effective in my job?" Listen carefully, and ask for context if it's not clear. **Stay curious and nonjudgmental.**

4. Replace an Old Habit with a New One

Take the habit or behavior you identified in #2 or #3 above and consider the cost of not making the change. Next, write down a small step you can take toward making the change, and identify an accountability partner (either a coach or trusted colleague) to support your effort.

5. Go Meta

Now, take a 30,000-foot view of yourself, and be as objective as you can. Did you really leave that last job because your boss didn't appreciate you? What may have been a contributing factor on your end in not getting that promotion? **Take stock and get real.** It's very useful to do a backward-looking career review every few years to gain the perspective that comes with time and experience. Are there any patterns emerging, and what lessons can you apply going forward?

In my experience, self-awareness is a gift to both yourself and others. It's a gift to yourself, because self-awareness is the root of all great personal satisfaction. It means you know why you do what you do and are clear in your beliefs. This clarity brings incredible external benefits, because you are viewed as an authentic leader who operates in alignment with your values.

Amii Barnard-Bahn
Executive Coach, Advisor, Author, Speaker
San Francisco Bay Area, California

Build a document or spreadsheet for yourself called an interface document, which can be used to show who in your organization is connected to each part of the ethics and compliance program. For example, when doing due diligence on third parties, there will be interfaces with procurement and supply chain, legal, business development, etc. This chart will help you quickly see who you need to speak to on matters that apply to your compliance program and where any communication or process gaps may be.

Amee Sandhu
CEO, Founder & Principal Lawyer
Toronto, Ontario, Canada

Consider Staffing Creatively

Are you a leader who, like everyone else these days, is trying to do more with less?

Maybe you're a startup owner trying to preserve working capital so you can grow your business without falling short of cash.

Or maybe you manage a team with a varied workload—sometimes up, sometimes down—and find it hard to hit the right staffing balance. Maybe you need that team to deliver on a bigger, more strategic project that takes dedicated focus, but they keep getting bogged down in day-to-day work.

If so, I want to let you in on a secret: **Stay-at-home moms who want to get back to work, even part-time, are some of the best resources money can buy.**

I should know. I built a company with some great ones!

And it's not just moms: Even today, five years past our founding, some of our top performers work part-time or flexible schedules. Some care for children. Others are aspiring authors or elite athletes.

My positive experiences with people looking for this kind of role has taught me a few things:

Flexibility can give you a discount on top-tier talent and experience. In a bootstrapping startup, any advantage is welcome. One of our first employees started working with me because she'd been laid off just before she returned from maternity leave.

A powerhouse talent with three kids under five, she deserved to do work at both the level and compensation she'd earned. But she needed a different life from the forty-plus-hour, in-office, always-on grind.

So we got an attorney with twelve years of experience who charged a project rate, allowing for predictable profit margins. And she got a flexible schedule with the ability to control her work. Win-win!

Your first ten hours are not the same as the last ten. Ten hours a week can sound negligible. Is a role that size even worth it? But you might be shocked at what a talented person can accomplish.

Most people who work full-time (me included) take coffee breaks or chat with co-workers or hop online to buy a gift or check personal email. I don't know anyone who sits down and just powers through each day, every day, without stopping.

But someone working ten hours per week with serious deliverables tends to be laser focused. They set dedicated time aside. When they work, they come in fresh, so ultimately, the time is worth more.

Remember that strategic project I mentioned? Getting someone focused on it for ten to fifteen hours each week can make the difference in driving things to completion.

It's not charity when it benefits you. Sometimes companies talk about hiring moms because it's the "right thing to do." And offering alternative work schedules is a powerful way to expand the hiring pool and send the elevator back down.

But what many companies don't realize is that offering flexible work can also benefit your bottom line.

When we were an early-stage company, hiring people who were paid hourly or by project—by choice—made it possible to flex our expenses with sales and cash flow. Years later, when the pandemic hit, that history of flexible work was a lifeline that let us adjust more quickly.

Flexibility with our payroll gives us flexibility as a company. Sure, it feels good to do it, but make no mistake: It's a benefit that benefits us, too.

Kirsten Liston
Principal & Founder
Westminster, Colorado

Curiosity, tenacity, creativity, and empathy are important for investigators. Being curious helps you look at all the angles of a potential issue and try to understand how and why it could happen.

Tenacity is digging for the truth and not just the easy answer.

Creativity is not only solving the problem, but designing the best solution so it won't happen again.

Empathy is being able to communicate with all parties involved in such a way that everyone from victim to suspect responds in the best way possible.

Whether I was on the employer side or defending a suspect, the best outcome was one that moved all the parties forward. You do that by trying to discover and report fully and completely. You can still be empathetic and impartial.

At the end of every day, most people want to look in the mirror and see a good person. Be the good person in your professional and personal life.

Kelly Paxton
Certified Fraud Examiner
Portland, Oregon

Chapter Seven

Talking To My Younger Self

Lisa says...

" One of the things I remember from my younger life is how I was never sure if I was as smart or qualified as other people in the room. I remember in law school, there was a guy who carried around a pocket-size U.S. Constitution and always spoke authoritatively in class, and I would not speak in class. Over time, I learned that everyone was nervous in class (including "Constitution Guy," who became a friend) and that finding my voice and focusing on the tasks I wanted to accomplish made me forget about all the other things.

If I could talk to that young woman, I would tell her three things.

Rule one: You are always smart enough and are always qualified to bring something to the discussion. Full stop.

Rule Two: In compliance (and in law), you often have to speak hard truths. Resistance from others to what you are saying is to be expected. Don't let resistance (or fear of it) keep you from saying what's necessary.

Rule Three: The "cerveza rule." A young woman applying for a job looks at all the qualifications, and if speaking Spanish is one of the qualifications, she may not apply if she does not speak the language. Meanwhile, a man will say I went to spring break in Cancún and ordered a *cerveza*. Why not apply? There is no reason not to take risks, especially when looking for new jobs, contacts, or learning opportunities.

So, younger selves, stand up, take a breath, and reflect on what you can and will accomplish, whether it's as a leader in a place where you used to sit in the corner, providing hard truths that make your organization better, or just being a little less hard on yourself on a bad day. Just like the women who share their stories below.

Don't Worry if You Don't Fit the Norm

If I could go back in time and give advice to my twenty-something self, it would be "don't worry if you don't fit the norm!" I remember when I first started working in compliance in the Washington, DC area, I would go to conferences and be one of the only young women in the room. Mostly, it was ex-security personnel who had come out of the FBI/CIA/police/military who were taking on this newer area of "compliance" for higher-risk industries that needed to respond to regulation. It seemed like a barrier was already in front of me to become successful in the field I had chosen. Fast-forward fifteen years, and I was a group compliance officer working among other great female compliance officers.

The population of women compliance officers from diverse backgrounds grows and encourages me every day. The change was, in my mind, organic, and I can't put my finger on any one thing that moved these goalposts. What I do know is that with a need for more proactive compliance programs, not just reactive ones, women around me are shaking up the norm in thinking creatively on how to create a culture of compliance that can be embedded in a company's DNA, rather than simply a policing department.

I work with compliance officers as a consultant now, across many industries and nationalities, and the number of strong women I have been able to work with is inspiring. There still appears to be a barrier for women at the board level in our industry, and when compared with their male counterparts, women in compliance roles can sometimes face discrimination for making strong decisions as required by their role, but I am optimistic that will continue to change. Don't conform with the norm, and you will find success!

Lauren Higgins
Consultant
London, United Kingdom

"

Be ready to speak truth to power. This is the hardest lesson to impart, particularly for an outside lawyer who doesn't have to interact each day with those people whom she might alienate by speaking truth. (I can always just stop working for a particular client. I still have my practice. I realize that it's a luxury in-house compliance professionals don't have.) But it's so important to be prepared to speak up when you need to.

Indeed, those women compliance officers I most admire, who are most successful, are those women who were able to act decisively when necessary.

Rebecca Walker
Compliance Lawyer
Santa Monica, California

"

The Power of Play

When I was four years old, I surprised my parents by learning to read by watching *Sesame Street*. Watching the show wasn't work for me, it was part of playing: games, humor, and joy.

Although I learned to read quickly, it took me many more years to understand the power of play. In the beginning of my career, I spent a lot of time being very professional and intellectual as I advised my in-house clients, drafted and negotiated multimillion-dollar contracts, and even changed a few laws.

There was a lot of work, but not a lot of play involved in the work. Then, around fifteen years into my career, I read Daniel Pink's *A Whole New Mind*, which predicted that play would become a more important factor in creating value in the 21st century. Pink said that play drives productivity and fulfillment, but I had not seen anyone apply the concept of play to the legal field.

There is a time and place for play; a courtroom or high-stakes negotiation would not be an appropriate opportunity, but maybe there were others. I was initially uncertain that play could be incorporated into serious topics like antitrust or anti-corruption.

On the other hand, if it could increase my impact as an in-house counsel, I was willing to try it. I started to experiment with the concept, and the results exceeded my expectations. Play brought legal advice to life through storytelling. Quizzes became games. Case studies became choose-your-own-adventure simulations. Employees became contributors and collaborators, not just audiences.

Employees who helped on projects became ambassadors and recruited others. Projects that incorporated play became viral. Before long, I had a waitlist of employees volunteering for legal and compliance projects. Employees understood and retained legal concepts more easily. Projects advanced at a quicker pace because people enjoyed contributing. Daniel Pink was right: The impact of play is phenomenal for all ages. If only I had realized this twenty years ago.

Kim Yapchai
Chief Compliance & Sustainability Officer
Lake Forest, Illinois

Finding your tribe means surrounding yourself with people who will support you, who want to see you succeed, and who have the courage to tell you the good and the bad, to stand with you, and to challenge you when you need it. You need to be the same to them. While no one can take better care of you than yourself, everyone needs help and support from others. No one makes it alone. Knowing your worth is especially important in the workplace.

Fabiana Lacerca-Allen
SVP & CCO
Hayward, California

Be Kind (Especially to Yourself)

I'm sure I am not the only one who's very demanding of herself. People often think that they are not good enough, that they don't deserve to be in the position they are in, and that they will eventually be "found out." It's called Impostor Syndrome, and it made me waste valuable time and emotional energy trying to cover for what I thought I was lacking relative to my peers. Trying to compare yourself with others is a killer.

One of my mottos is "Learn it until you know it," so I studied more, got a master's degree, obtained multiple professional titles, and was always the first person to put up my hand to take on additional responsibilities … I became an overachiever, but because I was always looking over my shoulder, waiting to be discovered as an impostor, I felt like I had to stay one step ahead to not get caught.

Twenty years later, I know that I bring something different to the table. The fact that I don't have the same set of competencies or qualifications as others is actually my value, and it's something that makes our team even stronger.

Patricia Alleyn
Head of Integrity Program
Montreal, Quebec, Canada

"

Do. Not. Engage. In. Gossip.

Just don't. It's not worth your time, nor your brain capacity; you're probably not getting the full story anyway, and one day that person will tell some other gossip to someone else, but it will be about you instead. The best thing is to ignore it. When I say "ignore it," I'm urging you to stop the person before they even tell you what it is all about.

By ignoring the gossip, you help in two different ways:

(1) You're sending a clear message that you think gossip is wrong. This will reverberate with people around you and your team.

(2) You're helping to stop a pervasive stereotype about women in professional settings.

Bonus: you use your brain capacity for productive matters! A win-win, in my view.

Fernanda Beraldi
Senior Director, Ethics & Compliance
Indianapolis, Indiana

"

Building Confidence Takes Time

Here's the advice I would give to myself fifteen years ago, when I was a brand-new big-firm lawyer who had just given birth to very premature twins being taken care of by a stay-at-home husband: be more assertive.

I had to find the tone that worked for me, first as a litigator and often the only woman in the room, and then with different kinds of operational, business, and management responsibilities. External forces worked against me, of course; many women must walk a fine line between being what, for a man, would be seen as passionate, but for a woman, can be viewed as shrill and aggressive. Or, maybe worse, turning a woman's rational argument into something emotional: "She's all worked up!"

Building confidence takes time, and my advice may have fallen on deaf ears in the early years of my career. I am a bit risk-averse (perhaps not surprising for someone who works in law and compliance), but the calculated risks I did take—such as asking for 80% time when I needed it, and changing careers—did work out.

I couldn't have known then that my three kids would be okay if I worried less, and that I could have stood my ground earlier and more often, whether it was in dealing with internal corporate politics or explaining (as Justice Ruth Bader Ginsburg had to do) to nurses and teachers that I am not the one at home during the day. It is okay that I am not the one responsible for dinner. (Will people ever stop commenting about RBG's cooking skills? I would like to know how well Antonin Scalia cooked for his kids.)

So often being "likeable" as a woman or being a "good mother" does not comport with being a business leader in a way that being "likeable" as a man or being a "good father" can. Sometimes, I learned, I had to let go of worrying about what other people think—while still staying true to my own values—to have my voice heard.

Rebecca Hughes Parker
Editor in Chief & Attorney
New York, New York

Don't Apologize for the Safety Vest

Based on my (very limited) research, women in the compliance field tend to be rule followers by nature. There's a reason compliance appeals to us. Don't apologize for it. Yes, we were probably the ones in elementary school who wanted to be the safety patrols and wear the orange vest. We were the ones in middle school who finished the group project when the other two kids failed to pull their weight, but we did it because we believe in getting the job done and doing it correctly. We don't tolerate people who don't get the rules and need to have them explained repeatedly.

Yet we find ourselves in a field where compliance violations occur usually because people don't follow the rules. It should be simple for them to understand, but it's not. Why don't people follow the rules? There's never a clear answer, and we desperately want to provide an answer.

Ambiguity makes us rule followers uncomfortable at best and intolerant at worst. Neither of those characteristics are great for success. Therefore, we need to learn to break down the problem. Why don't people follow the rules? It could be because they think the rules don't apply to them. Or they think they already know the rules, but what they really know is either an old rule or only part of the rule. Then, some people believe they are above the rules.

I wish someone had told me upon graduation from law school that even though we have a civilized society that operates on laws, rules, and social norms, more often than not, our chosen profession in the compliance field is replete with ambiguity.

If you don't know the answer right away, saying, "I don't know, I'll get back to you" really is a good response. In fact, it's the right response. I just wish I had learned that one sooner.

M. Beth Colling
Senior Vice President & Chief Compliance Officer
Boston, Massachusetts

"

I was only twenty-seven when I landed the position of regional compliance manager and became the youngest member of the management team. I was very excited about my position, but rather concerned about my age, and even started to wear glasses for important meetings to look older.

I came to my one-to-one with the regional CEO wearing my glasses, and because of his surprised look at me I explained the reason why I was wearing them. Probably after this meeting I noticed that he increased his public appreciation and support of the compliance function, so … in half a year, there was no need to wear my glasses anymore.

Elena Kovaleva
Compliance Officer
Dubai, UAE

Chapter Eight

Advice, Encouragement and Pep Talks

Remembering Why You Chose this Job in the First Place

Lisa says...

" I've had days where I have accomplished something I thought was impossible. Maybe I aced a presentation, came up with a solution to a tricky issue, or even managed to get a message across to increase a culture of compliance when I thought it would be a challenge. I try to remember those, because we all have so many of the other days...

You know what I'm talking about. Days when your project feels like you are pushing a rock up a mountain or when you end up with a new colleague or manager who changes your team dynamics in a negative way. And then there are the ones when you aren't being heard until someone else comes up with the "great idea" that just happens to be the same one you've been raising for days.

One of the biggest challenges I have experienced is when colleagues say what they think you want to hear from a legal and compliance standpoint just so they can move on to whatever they consider to be the business at hand—and ideally have you leave the meeting.

Those are some of the times I think about the pep talks and encouragement I've received. I still recall the first time I was the only woman in a meeting and, when the men indicated they were finished with the compliance portion, they said I could leave. Part of me wanted to, but it was important to stay, so I asked to stay to learn more about the transaction at hand. So, even if they hoped I would leave, I stayed. Not only did I get the chance to make sure they were going to take my views into account, I also learned more about the business and built relationships. It doesn't always turn out that way, but the stories I heard from others encouraged me that day.

So, don't forget: Even on the tough days, you have made it this far. You can handle the challenges. You've got this. You are in your role for a reason, and you deserve to be there, even when it feels like nothing will go your way. (It may not today, but there is always another day.)

And, as **Gwen Romack** and **Allison Watts** remind us later in this chapter, when you need some encouragement, reach out to someone—whether in your personal network or in our larger ethics and compliance community—because we all believe in YOU.

Send the Elevator Back Down

What an evocative metaphor, and what a timely topic.

Compliance may be a comparatively new profession, yet it is well enough advanced for us to know its significance for the sustained success of the organizations and broader society we serve.

As women in compliance, we consistently marvel at the cooperation and encouragement we have received from others in our burgeoning profession and its associated disciplines. This support has helped us secure a position of professional credibility from which we are now ready—and I believe obligated—to focus on the development of new entrants.

Having spent twenty-five years as a chief human resources officer before becoming a workplace ethics and anti-corruption compliance consultant, the elevator metaphor provides an ideal structure for the sharing of insights into how careers develop—particularly the careers of those who have been historically under-represented in the workplace.

The Privilege of Waiting for the Elevator

The next time you feel a touch of impatience as you wait for the elevator doors to clear, reflect on the life-changing significance that employment represents for so many. While there is widespread concern about the gap between the income of top executives and the average worker, there is also a chasm between the life circumstances of those who are unemployed and those who hold the most elementary of entry-level positions.

The most routine role represents an opportunity for career development that eludes the unemployed. When it is a woman holding that position, we know there is an additional benefit for society: Research indicates that the average woman spends a greater percentage of her income on the nutritional and educational needs of children than does the average employed man. For every dollar paid to a female worker, greater benefit is returned to society as a whole.

This is why we should not limit our efforts to the advancement of professionally qualified women. What is needed is our support for the increased percentage of women in any role at every level. Our future colleagues in compliance may well be among those who get their first foot in the door.

The Express Elevator Gets Stuck More Often

Pressured by both diversity targets and demands for advance identification of successors, it is easy to become enamored with the concept of "fast-tracking" career advancement.

In reality, the experiences bypassed by those with early evidence of high potential can be the cause of abrupt, unexpected career derailment. We can do a disservice to those we direct to the express elevator too soon; they miss opportunities to develop competencies such as resilience that are needed to succeed at the top, but which are typically acquired when facing the challenges found on the second or third floor.

In Praise of the Second Floor

No organization can cater to the aspirations of every employee. Why then do we not attach greater value to those with satisfied expectations—those deriving sufficient meaning and challenge from their roles and not aspiring to greater heights?

As we focus on the advancement of women in compliance, let's recognize and value every contributor rather than reserve our support for those with high levels of ambition. Where we can influence job content and project assignment, a focus on lateral (not just vertical) enrichment can add value to the work lives of all team members.

Personal circumstances can have a significant impact on our felt growth need and capacity. A colleague we had assumed would happily retire in a long-held role can surprise us by unexpectedly starting to seek greater challenge. Nurturing young talent is rewarding, but we shouldn't overlook the joy to be found in supporting a late bloomer.

Part Second Floor, Part Fourth Floor

In his early writing, management author Peter Drucker made the observation that where there are peaks, there are valleys, and that if you seek to employ candidates with no weaknesses, you may well find yourself surrounded by those with no strengths. It is also true that when overplayed, our strengths can become our weaknesses.

We make an invaluable contribution to the development of others when we encourage them to apply their strengths appropriately and assist them in identifying strategies to compensate for their areas of comparative weakness. This may mean holding up a mirror that they find difficult to look into. Done with the right intention, most recipients of your observations will be grateful for them, even if at the time their response is defensive.

Every Passenger Counts

It's a privilege to share in and add value to the career journeys of all we have the opportunity to impact. As you engage with the experiences and insights so generously shared on the pages that follow, you will marvel at the myriad of life experiences that characterize and influence any one career. May their truths inspire you to embrace the often challenging but always rewarding task of sending the elevator back down.

Penny Milner-Smyth
Organizational Behavior, Workplace Ethics
& Anti-Corruption Compliance Specialist
Durban, KwaZulu-Natal, South Africa

When I was a fifth-year associate, I was invited to speak at an international conference to help represent the "U.S. view" on combating corruption and to share insights on some recent developments in FCPA enforcement. It was my first time on a panel–ever–and I was easily the youngest person in the room. On stage, I was sitting next to a much more experienced attorney who had a similar area of expertise (if you could call mine "expertise" at that point).

I had carefully prepared for my assigned questions and brought written talking points on stage. In the first round of questions, the more experienced attorney, who was called on first, ended up saying the gist of what I had prepared, and I had to quickly come up with something to add when it came to my turn. Realizing what had happened, and probably seeing how nervous I was, the experienced attorney leaned over to me before the next round of questions and quietly said: "I see you've prepared a lot–you should speak first. I will find something to add afterward." When the next question was asked, the other attorney graciously gave me the floor and then publicly complimented my response.

It was a small gesture for the other attorney and incredibly powerful for me–both in the moment and even now, years later, as I think about how to create space for more junior colleagues to showcase their abilities.

Ann Sultan
Compliance & Investigations Attorney
Washington, D.C.

Compliance as a Second Language

Like many (most?) of us, **Melanie Sponholz** says she did not specifically set out upon a professional journey to become a compliance officer.

"I don't mean to denigrate the profession I now love, but let's be honest, when asked what I wanted to be when I grew up or when I graduated, 'compliance officer' was not on the tip of my tongue," she says.

Depending on which year you stopped the time machine, the answer could have ranged from veterinarian to Broadway star to chief operating officer. However, as seemed to happen to many of us, compliance serendipitously found me. Actually, I was initially "voluntold" to head up an organization's compliance program development, and I've never looked back.

Thus, when compliance found me, it was not my primary business language. Thankfully, my clinical, operational, and quality assurance vocabulary lent some sense of familiarity to the language of this new realm. At first I felt a bit like a foreign exchange student, plunked down amid conversations in which I understood about 60% of what was being discussed. How could I attain fluency—fast? Having learned from experience, I offer this advice on attaining compliance fluency to those of you who are new to the field:

Think back to middle school language classes. Memorizing vocab words and conjugating verbs will only get you so far in your efforts to converse. These academic exercises will not prime your neural pathways to think and speak in your new language. Instead, we go back to the example of a foreign exchange student: Immersion is key.

By surrounding yourself with dialogue in this new language and creating myriad opportunities to converse, you can gain fluency. Attend as many compliance conferences and events as you can. Join compliance groups and forums. Follow thought leaders and discussion groups on LinkedIn. Seek informative podcasts for your car rides and runs. Read and listen every day, until the words and sounds become familiar.

Of course, you'll need to join the conversations, too. No one's language skills were ever perfected without speaking! Too intimidated to pipe up in group settings? Find your own crew of compliance connections and create opportunities for one-on-one conversations to practice your skills. Build relationships with the authors, speakers, and fellow association members you encounter. Admiring an expert from afar? Reach out and introduce yourself! Find your own mentors at every turn! Compliance can be the land of Lone Rangers, so a sturdy contact list will be one of your best career resources.

During my first year as a compliance professional, I was lucky enough to encounter a group of New Jersey compliance leaders at the annual HCCA (Health Care Compliance Association) institute. Those generous souls (shout-out to the NJ HFMA CARE Forum!) took me under their collective wing and are my phone-a-friends to this day. Practice your conversational compliance with your new network.

One day, it will hit you: You are thinking and speaking fluent compliance like it's your job. Wait ... it is your job! What once seemed like a foreign language is now your second (or third or fourth) tongue.

Then think about paying it forward. Can you "host" a compliance "exchange student" yourself? Invite new members to the groups you belong to, or organize a new group. Offer your services as a sounding board and conversation partner. Don't limit your promotion of your new language to compliance colleagues. Share compliance conversations with teammates across all areas of your organization. The less foreign the dialogue of compliance seems, the more impactful we can be in our organizations.

Melanie Sponholz
Chief Compliance Officer
Chicago, Illinois

"

My advice for women in compliance is to be unapologetically smart and bold. Continue to study and learn your craft, challenge yourself to grow outside your comfort zone and try new specialties within compliance, and find great mentors and friends in compliance … it really does make all the difference. This is advice I still use myself.

Asha Palmer
Chief Ethics & Compliance Officer
Montclair, New Jersey

"

Trust Your Inner Self;
She Knows You Best

Gwendolyn Hassan started law school a little later in life than most. She tells us she was preparing to graduate at the age of 30 and was already married when she received a call to interview for an in-house position. She was excited about the opportunity and quickly agreed to come in for an interview.

Shortly after scheduling the interview, I learned my husband and I were expecting our first child. I was nervous, as the timing wasn't ideal. Would being pregnant negatively impact my ability to find a job? Would anyone hire a pregnant law school graduate who had yet to pass the Bar? How would I balance being a new attorney with being a new mom?

I had a great connection with the female general counsel I interviewed with. She was smart, candid, and warm. I told her I had just learned I was pregnant and wanted to be fully transparent with her. She was entirely unphased and, in fact, praised me for pursuing both a career and motherhood. She was downright effusive in her excitement for me and shared that she had her first child right out of law school as well. She was gracious and supportive and made me feel like being both a great mother and a great attorney at the same time was very possible.

I accepted the position, starting work when I was four months pregnant. My first day on the job started with orientation in the office of the VP of Human Resources, also a woman. She introduced herself and then unceremoniously announced, "So, I hear you're knocked up!" (Seriously, those were her exact words.)

I sat there, befuddled for a moment, unable to fully process what she had said to me. Finally, I managed to respond, "Well, my husband and I are expecting our first child in the fall, if that's what you mean." She responded by saying, "Well, if you want to doom yourself to doing a half-assed job of everything for the rest of your life, then I guess that's your choice," while she scoffed dismissively.

I was terribly confused, and my confusion must have shown on my face as she then continued, "Well, when you're at work you should really be at home with your child, and when you're with your child, you should probably be at work ... so, yeah, you will do a half-assed job of everything from now on ... good luck with that!" And the horrible thing was, she was completely serious.

I left her office in stunned silence, worried I had made a grave mistake in accepting the job. I found the nearest bathroom and had a good cry. I was shocked to hear these judgments from another professional woman. Aren't we supposed to be a sister-hood of sorts, lifting each other up and supporting each other? Why would she treat me that way? What did she have against me? She didn't even know me!

Also on my first day, I learned the general counsel I had such a great connection with had left the company. Had she already accepted her new role when she interviewed me? Did she say all those nice things to me because she wanted to get the open position filled before she left? When I pulled myself together and found my desk, I found a lovely vase of flowers and a handwrit-ten note from her, apologizing for not being there on my first day and encouraging me to never let anyone tell me that being a mother was in any way incompatible with being an amazing attorney. She said she knew I would have great success in my new legal career.

In the space of half an hour, I had been on a veritable rollercoaster of emotions (and not just because I was pregnant!) based not on anything objective, but rather on the words and opinions of two very different women who could not have been more diametrically opposed in their opinions of my life choices.

I am grateful for both of these women. Together, they taught me the very important lesson that there will always be people who criticize and underestimate you, and there will always be people who encourage and support you—often at the same time and based on the same set of facts. Everyone has their own personal agendas and perspectives. Many carry around chips on their shoulders we know nothing about. People make judgments about us and our competence and value, most often based on their own idiosyncrasies and foibles, not on our true merits. People's judgments of us usually reveal far more about how they feel about themselves than how they actually feel about us.

Especially working in a field like compliance, there will always be people who disagree, doubt, or question your wisdom. The key is not to buy into either the positive or the negative judgments others will make about you; rather, remain committed to your own internal sense of competence and self-worth. Being confident in what you have to offer means neither baseless criticism nor unmerited praise will sway or shape your perceptions of yourself. If you remain true to who you know you are, to what you know is right, then neither the critic nor the flatterer will have power over how you feel or what you can achieve. Trust your own voice!

Gwendolyn Lee Hassan
Director & Managing Counsel, Global Compliance
Oak Park, Illinois

There's a Lesson in Everything

Leadership can be lonely. The hard calls fall to you, and sometimes you'll have to communicate those decisions while meeting the eyes of the unfortunate recipients of your decisions. If you have a heart, it will hurt you. And it's not always clear whether your decisions are the right ones.

Jenny Kim shared that she's often asked, "what's next?" Her response is often "I don't know. But let's find out together. Instead of pontificating about what's next, let's discuss how to navigate what's next."

Without a crystal ball or a Ouija board, none of us can predict what's coming, and we can't control the unexpected.

However, we can control our reactions—whether we will convert that challenge into opportunity or that unknown person into a friend—and whether we keep moving forward in a positive direction. Four strategies to do that:

1. Listen to hear, not to respond. Listen for vocabulary and meaning. Just because you are all using the same words and acronyms does not mean you are all "speaking the same language." Remember, context is important—don't forget about Amelia Bedelia and how she interpreted words differently.

2. Say (and write) "thank you" often. No one ever does it alone. Someone in your life deserves to hear your appreciation—if only for standing by you through all your "ugly" and for making the team look good.

3. Take your work—but not yourself—seriously. Laugh a lot, especially at yourself. The good times won't last forever, and some humor will help to carry you through the difficult times.

4. Launder your heart daily. You cannot be effective when you hold onto the burdens and disappointments of the past. You will burn out if you don't figure out how to release them, because there will be many more ahead.

Savor each moment, and treasure each person who works with you; even if unpleasant, you can learn from each experience. As the song from *Sunday in the Park with George* states, "The choice may have been mistaken/The choosing was not/You have to move on."

Jenny Kim
Deputy General Counsel,
Political Law & VP, Public Policy
Washington, D.C.

Integrity Sometimes Comes at Great Personal Cost

When **Letitia Adu-Ampoma** shared her story with us, she described an image of a giant hammer poised to strike an egg. She offered encouragement to a young colleague who found herself under the "hammer" of an unscrupulous boss, yet "the egg did not crack."

She quoted Ralph Waldo Emerson in saying, "In failing circumstances, no one can be relied on to keep their integrity." Yet the anecdote she shared proves the opposite can be true.

Letitia's colleague, "Sarah," was a finance officer reporting to the head of the operation. This person wanted Sarah to onboard a third party, but due diligence revealed that the risk posed by the relationship—per her company's own policy— required approval from headquarters. She followed policy and forwarded the information to HQ, but received no response.

A month later, Sarah's boss asked her to send a payment to the third party, though there had been no approval and no contract. Sarah refused. Letitica describes what happened next:

Then the bullying began. The head of the operation called her out for not being a team player, downgraded her performance rating, and put her on a performance monitoring plan, all nicely documented and approved by HR. Sarah still did not make the payment. She resigned and left the company instead.

I contacted Sarah a few months after she left. She was facing a hard time personally and professionally, and she needed time to reflect. She had acted with integrity despite the failing circumstances around her, and she paid a heavy price for it.

I offered the best words of encouragement and commendation I could, which in the circumstances seemed pretty damned feeble! I also asked her how she found the strength to stand her ground and not be bullied into making the payment. Her next words shocked me.

"You were the only person I learned anything from in that company, even though I never worked for you. I watched how you stood out from all the other management, and I realized it was because you were transparent about your values. Everything you did or said supported them, and you never compromised yourself, even when everyone else wanted you to. You gave me the courage."

I had conflicting emotions, processing this. She may have done the right thing, but it was at great personal cost, and I had somehow contributed to what was a painful and traumatic time.

Sarah's experience taught me three things, which I carry with me every day:

1. Do not underestimate the power of example and what people may learn from you. Sarah never worked for me or reported to me. We just happened to be working in the same company at the same time.

2. Integrity should not come at a personal cost, but sadly it sometimes still does. What I can do for other women who experience this is help them turn the situation around.

3. In the context of international corporate scandals, do not be quick to believe the narrative of a "rogue country operation" with "rogue employees." It is a narrative comparable to rogue traders in investment banking scandals. The activities were likely known but ignored.

P.S., I am guessing many of you wonder what happened to Sarah. After resigning, she decided to take a yearlong sabbatical from work, after which she was still reluctant to take on a finance role in which she would have responsibility for payments. I challenged her to try other business roles and helped her secure her first consulting engagement on a business strategy project. Now I am just watching her fly!

Letitia Adu-Ampoma
Director
Ghana, West Africa

It's a Small World, After All

Next, **Barbara Boehler** takes us on a tour of compliance careers, welcoming us with:

"It's a Small World" is not only a ride in Fantasyland with an annoyingly catchy melody (It's going to be stuck in your head now, too. Sorry.), it's also an observation I find myself making with incredulity, nearly constantly.

The phrase is often repeated as a caution, as in, "Be sure to practice the golden rule, because it's a small world, and you never want to burn bridges." (How many folksy idioms can we cram into one sentence?) Rather than the small size of the compliance community underscoring this sternly worded warning, however, think of "it's a small world" as a tremendous opportunity to invest in relationships.

You may not know how many degrees of separation you are from Kevin Bacon, but if you have spent any length of time in the practice of compliance, it's likely you can claim a closer connection to a shockingly high number of compliance leaders in your industry. This phenomenon is proven within the digital pages of LinkedIn. Rather than just trying to amass great numbers of connections on LinkedIn, focus on having great connections. You don't get points for having more connections than anyone else does on the networking site, but there are incredible benefits to building a strong compliance community of peers and embracing the small world of compliance.

There's So Much That We Share ...

I'm going to go out on a proverbial limb by stating that, on occasion, the job of being a compliance officer is no day at the amusement park. I've found it can be helpful during those challenging times to have people in your corner who just "get it." And while we know that there are no "no's" in compliance, sometimes the answer is not what your co-workers want to hear. Let's face it: It's hard to be the bearer of news that no one wants to hear.

Having a contingent of folks who understand the unique challenges of the job is immensely helpful. Your compliance connections can give you peace of mind and offer practical advice and professional guidance to enhance not only your compliance program, but also your compliance career path.

I have found that those in the compliance community (GWIC, anyone?) are more than willing to share best practices and lessons learned. They give of their time and their expertise while sharing the practical stuff: their contacts, good articles, job postings, and sometimes excellent candidates. They provide information to guide others in enhancing their programs and professions. And—while there is no expectation of a quid pro quo—this is where the golden rule comes into play: This kind of sharing can only be discipline-enhancing and elevating.

When the kind and generous lady in the car in front of me at the Dunkin' Donuts drive-thru paid for my coffee, I happily got on board and paid for the coffee of the person next in line (even though she had honked at me because I was too slow moving up the line). As a side note: Be careful who you honk at—metaphorically, of course.

... That it's Time We're Aware

So, how do you build (and join) this strong network of compliance professionals? How do you become part of the small world of compliance? How do you amass your thousands of LinkedIn connections into a close-knit, integral compliance fellowship? Much like Rome, a strong community of compliance peers was not built in a day. This advice may seem commonsensical, but most compliance advice is rooted in common sense.

It's a Small World After All

Consider the following actions to help to enhance your compliance network:

1. **Join stuff:** What is the preeminent organization within your compliance specialty or industry?

2. **Attend stuff:** Attend conferences either virtually or in person, local or international. Seek out industry groups in your specialty within your city; if there isn't one, consider starting one.

3. **Read stuff:** Stay on the cutting edge of your industry or specialty. Know what is affecting your industry and peers.

4. **Participate in the conversation:** Use social networks to enhance the discipline, not break it down.

5. **Give back:** Whether it's coffee at the drive-thru, a kind word, or a good opportunity, use what is at your disposal to give back to the community.

Finally: Keep in touch. Cultivate your network. Remember your co-workers, both current and former. With just a little work, you can develop an enviable bench of strong compliance officers who will support you through the inevitable challenges—whether you're facing problematic regulatory change or a difficult career decision.

With the right team in your corner, you can sit back and enjoy the ride.

Barbara Boehler
Adjunct Lecturer
Boston, Massachusetts

It's important to never engage in a personal feud with anyone at the company. The compliance function is about integrity and doing what is right. It's normal for some people to be uneasy about the compliance program because they believe it will slow down the business.

Some detractors might just be afraid of the change that comes with compliance programs. You should communicate frequently with these people and address their concerns; winning them over is part of your job. However, people who attack you personally are bullies. Don't let these people put you down or demean your work. Your company should have a code of conduct that forbids any type of bullying. Make sure to report such behavior.

These tips are easier said than done, but as Eleonor Roosevelt famously said, "the way to begin is to begin."

Maria Monica Morris
Latin-American Compliance & Investigations Counsel
Bogota, Colombia

The Job She Didn't Think She Wanted

Kim Yapchai's first compliance position was an involuntary one. She was an assistant general counsel during the recession in 2009, and company staff had been cut in half.

"As a result, I found myself leading the compliance program," she says. "Truthfully, I was not excited about it. It was not seen as a good opportunity in the law department at that time. What I did not realize was how compliance would open up so many more possibilities for my career."

Here's what Kim did when faced with an unexpected turn of events:

First, I made it my mission to change the content and image of the program. I approached it as marketing for the law department in order to get employees to ask important questions and raise concerns. Like a product quality program, if we could catch defects when they were small and internal, or even avoid them, we could decrease the negative impact on the company.

I soon found that there was not much difference between being an assistant general counsel and a chief compliance officer. In both roles, I was advising employees to make decisions that follow the law—and dealing with the impact when they did not.

The key in choosing a compliance position is finding the right company. At many companies, a chief ethics and compliance officer role is similar to the general counsel. The breadth of the role and the types of laws you encounter through investigations, training, and controls is broad: FCPA, OFAC, antitrust, privacy, accounting fraud, SEC matters, employment, etc.

You set strategy and leverage your executive presence in interaction with the C-suite and the board of directors, often during a crisis. You also help to build the culture of the company by promoting the company values. As a result, I have found that it has broadened my potential career path rather than narrowed it. In addition to the succession plan for the general counsel, I have found myself on the succession plan for the chief human resources officer, as well as leading an environmental, social and governance program.

Now, when someone asks me whether they should consider a role in compliance, I highly recommend it. It's a great way to advance your skills to prepare for a C-suite role and have a positive impact at your company and around the globe.

Kim Yapchai
Chief Compliance & Sustainability Officer
Lake Forest, Illinois

"

Compliance is a very niche, complex, and highly dynamic area to work in, and a very prestigious one at the same time. It's not surprising, then, that skills in this domain are and will always remain in high demand. But in order to stay relevant and even ahead of the curve, keep learning. Regulations are rapidly changing and so is technology; a contextual understanding of both will ensure you stay at the top of your game.

And while you are at it, create a strong next layer that can support you and grow along with you. As women join the workforce and begin to grow in their careers—moving from trainees to leads to managers—they also often start their families as well, with responsibilities increasing personally and professionally at the same time. My advice to aspiring women leaders is to find a balance that can reduce conflict between work and family, create a support network, and leverage your organization's initiatives to support women in the workplace.

Sujata Dasgupta
Global Head, Financial Crimes Compliance Advisory
Stockholm, Sweden

A Job for the Long Haul

If you've ever been challenged to explain what you do for a living, you'll appreciate the way **Lisa Babin** describes a compliance career in terms of the role, the responsibilities, and the rewards.

I've always had a tough time describing my job to people outside of the corporate compliance world. Was I internal affairs? A preacher of corporate morality? A policy wonk? The cultural standard bearer? My son, as a little boy, just fueled my frustration with his question, "If you're an appliance manager, shouldn't our family have a nicer refrigerator?"

However precious that question was in the moment, it gave me much to think about over the years. Now, at a time when our political leaders take to task, marginalize, ridicule, or—worse—punish those who speak up for and stand with truth and fairness, the job description of the compliance leader is crystal clear.

The role of the compliance professional is distinct from that of the attorney or HR professional, who also play key roles in protecting and defending our companies. After all, attorneys who handle issues as complex and diverse as privacy and anti-corruption are instrumental in building a strong, rules-based corporate culture. They establish the legal goalposts that protect the company's values, brand, and reputation. Similarly, HR professionals, who support our employees, handle some of the most serious matters of our times, including harassment and discrimination. Both of these jobs are significant, and their responsibilities are weighty, and our companies rely on their expertise to protect and fortify them.

Compliance professionals also establish goalposts, set up guard-rails (a.k.a., compliance programs), and support and attend to employee issues. But their role is distinct from the others. As is the job of a parent, the compliance professional's most basic role is to lay the foundation of the company culture with the building blocks of company principles, standards, practices, and programs.

They also communicate with employees about company values, use their clear and unwavering voice to speak up for what's right, and help employees speak their own truths. At the same time, however, they have their ears to the ground, listening for rumbles to detect fault lines. To pull all of this together, the compliance professional helps the company and its employees navigate their challenges, the bumps in the road, and the near falls off the cliff. When they can't prevent the initial fall, they take action to prevent the next one. Just as with the job of the parent, the compliance professional's job grows in importance as the company matures and new challenges arise. It's a job for the long haul.

In my career, I have led many compliance investigations, but I've also been called upon to support investigations led by the HR and security teams. In those cases, the lead investigator conducts a thorough investigation of the allegations, delving into what was said, what was done or perceived to have been done, what was reported, and what outcomes resulted from the alleged behavior. The investigator may not always establish facts that link the evidence at hand to the allegations; in those cases, he or she may conclude that the allegations are unsubstantiated.

But as a compliance professional, with my eyes peeled and ears to the ground, I ask different questions. Why were these allegations made to begin with? What underlying factors or trends led to the behaviors we identified? In a recent investigation, for example, while the allegations were unsubstantiated, I found that the fear that the complainant would lodge a hotline complaint was overwhelming—so much so that the subject of the complaint (her leader) failed to take any meaningful action to address her performance issues, which in the end, led to her lodging a hotline complaint, the very thing he feared.

This was where I listened to the rumblings and connected the dots. Instead of concluding with an unsubstantiated allegation and no corrective action, I shed light on what led to the hotline call and brought the teams together to address the underlying (serious) issue in front of us: the deep-seated fear in that office of the whistleblower.

As we all know, compliance professionals cannot prevent all wrongdoing, no more than parents can prevent their kids from ever making mistakes or getting into trouble. But they can have a finger on the pulse of the organization, be on the lookout for the fault lines, and bring issues into the light to be grappled with, confronted, and acted upon—before the unthinkable happens.

At this point in my career, no one will confuse me with an appliance manager. I still don't have that fancy refrigerator, but I am proud to be among the community of compliance professionals. I know that now, more than ever, championing the importance of speaking up and speaking truth is front and center for the future of our families, our companies, our communities, our environment, our country, and the world as we want it to be.

Lisa Schor Babin
Global Compliance & Ethics Leader
Glen Rock, New Jersey

Be vulnerable. Admit when you do not know the answer, promise to find out, and then do it. Make connections and ask for advice. Most people will gladly share their stories. Worst case? They say no. Keep asking, and likely the next person will say yes.

Michelle Beistle
Chief Ethics, Compliance & Privacy Officer
Fairfax, Virginia

5 Things To Do
(Not Including Stress-Eating Twizzlers)

The final pep talk of the day comes from **Gwen Romack** and **Allison Watts**, a mentor-mentee duo for going on twenty years now. They describe themselves as "people who've been there: through the good, the stress-eating, and the ugly."

They also point out that a mentee can teach a mentor just as much as the reverse.

Here are a few things they've figured out along the way ... together.

And by the way:

"We're not going to tell you who is offering which piece of advice, because (1) we both whole-heartedly agree with all of it, and (2) this allows us to attribute the embarrassing stories to each other if you bring it up at a conference."

1. Kick perfectionism to the curb.

Despite being a lifelong high-performing go-getter, I can admit it: There will be failures.

I've learned that expecting perfection basically leaves you with two options: You can do everything right on the first try (yeah, right!) or you can not even bother trying. I discovered early on that doing everything perfectly on the first try doesn't often happen, but it wasn't until much later that I learned it's okay to make mistakes—and even fail.

Learning to be resilient is critical for growth, and the sooner you learn that, the faster you'll grow. Early in my career, I labored over every single assignment and every email (a.k.a. "perfection paralysis"). I'm talking, in the office until midnight, eyes half shut, trying to make sure that everything was 100% perfect. And no matter how much time I spent, it never was.

I was saved from myself by (1) seeking out a mentor and (especially) (2) learning to strive for a "what's best for now" solution instead of perfection.

The saying "you are your own worst critic" couldn't be truer. There is always room for improvement, but if you keep spinning your wheels trying to make something 100% perfect, you'll never get that instant feedback—the real stuff that helps you learn and grow. So put the quality effort in and move on to the next task or project. If you're met with critical feedback or even failure, don't let it break you, let it shape you into what you want to be!

2. Get the certifications.

There are a lot of views on the value of professional certifications. I myself have found some to be a lot of work for a whole lot of *meh*, but I've always come away having learned something new. Always.

Certifications have helped me to think differently. My early certification work around process and quality improvement taught me how to look at things critically and find ways to create incremental improvements, test them, reset, and try again. It also taught me that failing isn't bad, as long as you fail fast and keep learning.

My project management certification provided a totally different lens. And later, my compliance- and risk-related certifications gave me the broad and deep knowledge I needed to really "get it" at a holistic level. They got me thinking outside of my specific industry and my big corporate experience to incorporate lots of different vantage points. I've also used them over the years to maintain brain cells, lead by example, and learn new things.

Certifications have often helped me connect previously (often embarrassingly) unconnected dots, too.

Here's an embarrassing example you have to promise not to tell. When I was studying for the CCEP exam, I was more than a few years into a great compliance career, with tremendous experiences in lots of areas and situations at a very large multinational tech company. I'd probably made more than 100 audit committee slide decks for my bosses, so I had a vague idea of the purpose of their presentations. As I studied for the exam, I read an article that broke down the role of the board, how it works via committees, and their responsibilities. I had a ten-years-too-late lightbulb moment about what exactly the audit committee is and how it plays into an effective compliance program! This leads me to our next piece of advice …

3. Find someone you can ask really dumb questions.

After my "ohhh, thaaaaat's what an audit committee is" revelation, I realized that my knowledge about some things had been limited to the topics my bosses and mentors had shared with me. I then began sharing my little revelations with my team (which sometimes led to shock and laughter) and encouraging them to ask me ANY dumb question.

Find someone you trust who you can ask any question and not worry they'll judge you. And, when you can, show your team you're that person for them. And in case you're wondering how I could go so long and high in a career without understanding the board structure, please know I was twenty-three when I realized a pickle was a cucumber that had been pickled.

I'll just add here, find someone who will tell you the unvarnished truth. For me, it was my so-called "mentee." I needed to be told when I was going off track or being too wound up. I needed to hear when I was losing perspective during stressful situations.

I trusted her implicitly to understand the moving parts of the situation, understand me, be my sounding board, and gently nudge (read: smack) me when needed.

4. Set wildly unrealistic career goals.

I stumbled on a career development packet from corporate America, circa 2000, that asked job seekers, "What is the highest-level job you hope to obtain in your career?" Having had little to no exposure to the choices, the requirements or the possibilities, I wrote down, "business process analyst." At the time, that role was TWO WHOLE levels above where I was. Gee, I was really aiming high, huh?

If someone had said to me then that I'd get to Senior Director at a Fortune 50 company, I would've been sure they were crazy. Our advice isn't just to set unrealistic goals, of course, but to discover your possibilities. Never miss a chance to interview (formally or informally) people in other departments and roles. Find out what they do, how, and what skills or education they need to do it well. Actively expand your awareness of the universe of jobs available to yourself and your teammates. Share that information. Then set your focus on the job you want three to five years from now and start working toward it. Do rotation assignments, volunteer on projects in that area, get that cert, network.

5. Change is the only constant, so learn to adapt!

I'm a planner by nature, so I like to think through and organize things. It takes time, but I'm always thoughtful and thorough when putting together project plans, business plans, and similar documents. Early in my career, I remember managing a fast-moving, multipronged project with a super-aggressive due date. I mapped it all out, making sure I's were dotted and T's were crossed.

Well, as you know—things happen. There were budget cuts, leadership changes, budget surpluses, technical issues, etc. Virtually everything that could possibly interfere with my project did. Frustratingly, my executive sponsor would say, "can't you just rethink and redo the plan with this in mind?" I've always believed that I bring flexibility to the table (please don't picture me attempting yoga!). Adaptability has taken time to develop, but it has paid off in spades.

What's the difference, you say? Flexibility is a willingness to meet someone halfway, whereas adaptability is a willingness to change your own ideas or presumptions, to be open to things, especially outside your comfort zone. Those rotation assignments mentioned earlier? DO THEM!! It's easy to stay inside your comfort zone and resist things that require you to step outside of it. If you're not ready to take that leap, start off by stretching yourself in small ways. Once you begin to let go, you'll handle change with so much more grace and ease.

6. Manage stress effectively.

I know, this is a sixth thing… While we make some light of it, in all seriousness, figure out how to manage stress in a healthy way—one that doesn't involve binge-eating Twizzlers. Compliance careers are stressful by nature. There's so much you'll be responsible for while having such little control.

No matter how well you train on, remind people, and implement internal controls to mitigate a risk, it's gonna happen. You may also manage difficult investigations of people you once respected, make difficult decisions without concrete information, provide assurances to leadership based on your best assessment (which you know is based on flawed and complex data), deal with subpoenas or regulatory oversight, make decisions about consequences that alter a person's life, convince employees at all levels to embrace compliance, stay tuned in to the latest prosecutions, and keep your team pressing on despite interdepartmental tensions. And that will just be a Tuesday.

For many of us, that will be happening at the same time as ailing parents, meal planning, laundry, and getting kids in the right clothes to the right place with the right sports gear.

So, find a confidante you can trust to talk through things. Find a physical outlet if you can (exercising, screaming into a pillow, a three-minute dance break in the ladies room, etc.). Find things you can do to release the stress and re-center. I wish I'd figured that out 7,456 Twizzlers and three dress sizes ago.

Gwen K. Romack
Ethics, Compliance & Anti-Corruption Leader
Washington, D.C. Area

Allison W. Watts
Associate Director, Ethics & Compliance
Program Management
Cumming, Georgia

Chapter Nine

Gratitude: Paying Tribute to Mentors

" It's fitting that some of the last entries in this book should be expressions of gratitude. Success rarely happens in a vacuum. If we are lucky, we are lifted from our earliest days by gracious professionals who pour into us time, encouragement, advice, and wisdom.

Some call these people mentors, some sponsors, some advocates, but all of them are a part of your team. I call it my "kitchen cabinet," and I am fortunate to have people that fall into all of these categories. Whatever you call the ones who've helped you on your professional journey, their impact is no doubt unmistakable.

Mary and I have both had many mentors, but a few stand out. She developed her professional relationship with **Tom Fox** in a similar way as I did mine with **Ellen Hunt**: We just reached out to them, and they supported us in our compliance journeys. For that, we will always be grateful.

Here, some of our contributors salute the mentors who've supported them on their own compliance journeys. These women and men have been faithful to send the elevator back down, and some Great Women in Compliance have developed as a result. **"**

The Idol Turned Sponsor

When I started out doing anti-corruption work ten years ago in Singapore, I was fortunate enough to have a senior compliance counsel show me the ropes and lay down a basic understanding of compliance knowledge. When she left the company, I looked to other avenues to build on my new skill set.

I came across **Tom Fox**'s blog, written from the other side of the world, and voraciously read the frequent postings, bolstering my confidence in the subject matter of this relatively newly enforced discipline.

Initially, I worked in small firms and didn't always get a chance to practically apply what I had learned from him, but by the time I did work at a company big enough, I knew how to apply the theory bestowed upon me by Tom.

I would eventually come to meet my idol at a conference (cue excited squealing and fangirling). Fast-forward to the future, and I now have a feminist podcast on Tom's Compliance Podcast Network. Not only did the guy who taught me the theory of compliance lay down that core information, he then also became an amazing sponsor of Lisa Fine and me, hosting the podcast on his network and giving us tips and tricks for how to release a successful compliance podcast.

Speaking of podcasts, Tom has now turned his hand to producing more podcasts than he does blog posts on compliance. He's prolific and covers a great deal for the modern compliance practitioner to learn from. The kindest part of all of this is that it's complimentary for the compliance community.

Along the same vein is Tom's care in making his thought leadership completely accessible. It's so generous! Not only does he not charge for much of it, but he also takes care to write in a way that is compelling for the typical layperson, not just veteran lawyers. In addition to the freely available material, Tom has also written countless books, including a textbook. Somebody give this guy a medal!

Mary Shirley
Head of Culture of Integrity and Compliance Education
Boston, Massachusetts

The E&C Sage

I have a wonderful network, and I have mentors from my early years in law firms through today. One person has been my mentor, sponsor, and greatest cheerleader. That's **Ellen Hunt**. Not only is she a consummate ethics and compliance professional, she also gives spot-on advice and support. But, even more important, she listens. And she truly cares—about doing the right thing and about the people who get the tangible and intangible benefits of having a robust and innovative compliance culture.

Ellen was my first interview for the Great Women in Compliance Podcast, and it was as I was getting to know her. I had also reached out to her to talk about my career and what I wanted to do going forward. She helped me crystallize my thoughts and allowed me to talk through my thought process, even when it meant taking time out of her extremely busy day.

She has given me a few bits of advice that I want to share:

- Be prepared to do the right thing, even if it means saying the unpopular thing or walking away;

- It is always possible to innovate to grow your program— whether in training, board presentations, or your own communications and code, and;

- Think bigger. Do not be the person who holds yourself back because you don't think you're ready. You are ready.

Thank you, Ellen, for being my advocate, champion, and friend. My career and my life are better for knowing you and learning from you.

Lisa Fine
Director of Compliance
Washington, D.C.

Standing on the Shoulders of Giants

… The timing of my entry into the compliance field was partially due to some old-fashioned good luck, but perhaps more importantly, the fact that I was in a position to capitalize on that good luck because I had a number of mentors and clients over the years who had taken a chance on me and my little solo practice when faced with some of their companies' worst obstacles (and potential bet-the-company litigation or enforcement action). Every step built upon the last. One referral from a female mentor turned into another and then another. I will not ever lose sight of the fact that to this day, I continue to stand on their shoulders.

Realizing that others had trusted me with these opportunities—and thus paved the way for me to help blaze the trail to establish compliance and ethics as a profession in Canada—made me determined to send the elevator back down every opportunity I could. I have strived to give opportunities to those who perhaps didn't show "on paper" the correct skill set for a compliance practitioner, but who impressed me with their humility or personal integrity or pragmatism. I have asked non-litigators to assist in investigations simply because they demonstrated a tenacious, dogged determination to figure things out or attack an issue from a creative or innovative angle. I have hired new grads, young moms, non-lawyers and some amazing women who otherwise would have left the legal profession altogether due to frustration with traditional practice.

I think we need to hire women with potential, help to develop them, and then get the heck out of their way. This is how we advance women, narrow the gender divide, and create leaders who hopefully go on to repeat the cycle.

Kristine Robidoux
QC, Senior Compliance & Regulatory Counsel
Calgary, Alberta, Canada

The Encourager

I've had a good mix of strong leaders—and frankly, quite terrible bosses who taught me what not to do—and for them I am grateful. That was valuable information! The manager who stands out most in terms of inspiring me to feel confident about my abilities and pushing me to do better has been **Mark Stanley**, currently SVP General Counsel at Fresenius Medical Care Asia-Pacific.

Mark is someone who instills a great deal of trust in his team members and doesn't micromanage, which I think we all know is a sign of a toxic culture. He is also someone I can turn to for answers when I am faced with a perplexing challenge I've not come across before and can't figure a way out of. However, for the purposes of this book, I'm going to focus on the nontechnical things I've learned. If you want to learn from Mark substantively, apply to be on his team!

Things I learned from Mark:

- It is entirely possible to coach your team on their weaknesses without them feeling you are criticizing them or even noticing in the moment that they are being coached.

- Be affable—always.

- Do what's right for your employees, even if it isn't the best move for you.

A friend of mine interviewed for a job on Mark's team a few years ago, and she reported back to me that when I had arisen in the discussion, Mark had said, "She is excellent. One day soon, she will be my competition." I think that's the best compliment I could have received from Mark and equally the best lesson learned: Forget about hierarchy, focus on ability, and always build up other people.

Mark, thank you for your mentoring and continued sponsorship. I am privileged to know you.

Mary Shirley
Head of Culture of Integrity and Compliance Education
Boston, Massachusetts

The Ethics Champion

"I've learned that people will forget what you said, people will forget what you did, but people will never forget how you made them feel." This familiar quote by Maya Angelou succinctly sums up interactions with **Tom Costa**.

Tom was my manager when I first ventured into compliance ten years ago at Bristol Myers Squibb. He was Vice President of U.S. Compliance and Ethics, and he patiently and productively developed and counseled me on the intricacies of health care law compliance, as well as the art of learning how to work to live, as opposed to living to work. Not only was Tom the best manager I ever worked for, he was a leader in the truest sense of the word. His commitment to ethical leadership was unwavering, and he was a champion for women in a world that, at times, was still dominated by men. Tom continues his important work today as a member of the Sanofi U.S. board of directors. As I have moved onto various roles and companies since working for Tom, he continues to be a trusted friend and mentor. I may never rise to the level of a Tom Costa, but I hope that along the way I can help others the way he has helped and continues to help me.

Amy Pawloski
Life Sciences Compliance Executive
Philadelphia, Pennsylvania

Mentors from Many Corners

I was very lucky to have many generous mentors throughout my career who gave me the gift of their time, whether it was a quick coffee or many one-on-one meetings. As a result, I always say "yes" when someone has the confidence to ask me for my time to talk with them about career advice. "Paying it back" has enriched my life in ways I never expected by creating connections to people throughout our profession.

Michelle Beistle
Chief Ethics, Compliance & Privacy Officer
Fairfax, Virginia

The Compliance Fairy

I started my career in finance at Microsoft Russia, and at that time I'd never heard of the compliance function. Our regional compliance manager sat not very far away from me, so I had a chance to observe some cool stuff she was doing—kind of like detective work—by reviewing an employee's expense reports, meeting various employees from very different departments and levels, doing training, performing investigations, and knowing all the secrets. She made me fall in love with compliance.

In 2010, in one of our career-building trainings, I stated my dream job: "I want to be a compliance manager." My life changed dramatically.

In three years, my dream came true! I was promoted to compliance manager for GE Healthcare CIS, being the youngest among my peers. I owe great appreciation to **Julia Mikhailova**, as well,

138

a compliance fairy who inspired me on this journey! We were able to reshape the compliance culture in the organization by receiving incredible support from my incredible regional CEO, **Olivier Bosc**, and my amazing manager, **Marcos Sanz**!

Elena Kovaleva
Compliance Officer
Dubai, UAE

The Two-Star General

Leadership is about putting others before yourself, establishing and promoting trust and loyalty, and being a lifelong learner, because no one does it alone.

When I first joined the Missile Defense Agency as a Presidential Management Fellow, my first rotation did not go so well. Within three months, I raised my hand and asked HR for a new rotation assignment, and they gave me one, assigning me to the department of the late retired Rear Admiral **David M. Altwegg**.

I had heard quite a bit about Mr. Altwegg—that as a retired two-star admiral, he was demanding, direct, and forceful. When I entered his office for our first meeting, I maintained a pleasant, noncommittal expression.

Our relationship began with a short conversation:

Mr. Altwegg: So, I have not read your resume.

Me: That's OK. There is not much to read on there. You're not missing anything.

Mr. Altwegg (eyebrows arched): Oh? And you're a lawyer?

Me: I just passed the bar. That does not mean anything. I am still learning.

Mr. Altwegg (leaning back in his chair, hands clasped above his head): Well, you're a PMI (Presidential Management Intern, the position's name originally), so you need to learn and to follow me around. I will take you to every meeting.

Me (very politely, but not believing him): That would be great. Thank you. I will stop wasting your time and I will work with your assistant to figure out your schedule. Thank you for the opportunity.

And there, our first conversation ended. I still think about that to this day.

Mr. Altwegg opened every door imaginable for me. He took me to every meeting, including ones with all the senior officials, made sure that I sat at the table and was treated like a colleague, rather than an "intern" or a "fellow," and ensured that I had the opportunity to serve at the White House Office of Counsel to the President.

Before I even believed in myself, for some reason, Mr. Altwegg believed in me, and he encouraged me to explore every avenue possible. He opened his contact list to me and made introductions. Those introductions led to my later positions at Crowell & Moring, Miller & Chevalier, and finally, my present position.

And he did not do this just for me, but for anyone he believed in.

To this day, I strive to do the same for my team and others around me who seek opportunities and counsel. True leadership is recognizing the talent around you and doing everything to help that talent grow, even if it means they leave you.

I can never repay the late Mr. Altwegg, but I can pass on his boundless generosity and wisdom to others.

Jenny Kim
Deputy General Counsel,
Political Law & VP, Public Policy
Washington, D.C.

The Long-Time, Ardent Supporter

I want to pay tribute to **Bruce Ambeault**, VP of Commercial Operations and the lead negotiator, contract drafter, proposal strategist, etc., to whom I was seconded from 2006 to 2011. I was asked by my employer's general counsel, Allan Hawry-luk (another wonderful mentor) to take a secondment in the commercial operations group after I had been in-house legal counsel for four years. It was exciting, but I was thrown into the deep end. In fact, during the first week I went to work with Bruce, he left on a business trip that was supposed to be for one week. It turned into six months.

He was a difficult person to work with, by his own admission, due to his exacting high standards and his way of telling you directly what was wrong with your work when it did not meet this standard. But we hit it off so well that we worked together for five years.

It was hard. I wanted to quit many times. He pushed his team to their limits and beyond. On the other hand, he always supported, defended, and shielded his team from others. He appreciated the efforts we made, gave us room to make mistakes as we learned, and was always there to push us to be our best. He will never agree with you just to be polite; he forces you to be compelling and persuasive, and if you persuade him, he will tell you.

He and I went our separate work ways almost ten years ago, but I still call and text him when I need wise counsel. He and his wife might dislike the intrusion on their retirement, but if they do, they never show it!

Amee Sandhu
CEO, Founder & Principal Lawyer
Toronto, Ontario, Canada

The Four-Leaf Clover

I first met **Bobby Kipp** in 2012, when she hosted a local round-table to discuss the results of PwC's compliance benchmarking survey with *Compliance Week*. Later that same year, she and I moderated back-to-back plenary sessions at the Ethics and Compliance Officer Association's 20th annual conference. I never would have imagined that, a mere year later, I would have the incredible opportunity to work alongside Bobby—to learn from her, to befriend her, and to emulate her in years to come.

Bobby was a founding member of what started as the Ethics Officers Association (and then became the ECOA, now the ECI), and she was the first Chief Ethics Officer in the public accounting industry. She is an absolute legend in the field, though I don't believe she got anywhere near as much credit as she deserved. I suppose the verb tense that I have chosen may make it seem as if Bobby has left this world. In fact, just the opposite is true. In

2016, she retired from PwC—and early, may I add. Now Bobby is living life to its fullest, playing her oboe, singing in a choir, skiing in winter, playing tennis year-round, enjoying time with her family. And, of course, inspiring jealousy in those of us still toiling away in the workplace!

Jealousy is only one of many things that Bobby inspires in me— and many others. As a boss, she inspired loyalty. As a colleague, she motivated me to be better. As a mentor, she encourages me to believe in myself. And, to quote an Irish proverb, as a friend, she is like a four-leaf clover: hard to find and lucky to have. I would have neither succeeded nor survived at PwC without Bobby, and I was both humbled and honored when she asked me to give a speech at her retirement party.

To put it simply, I was devastated when Bobby retired. True to form, however, Bobby may have left PwC, but she didn't leave me. I am fortunate that she is still in my life; in fact, we'll be at a Zoom cocktail party later this evening! So, I want to take this opportunity to say THANK YOU, Bobby, for everything that you did for me, your co-workers, and the compliance and ethics community at large. We are all the better for knowing you.

Andrea Falcione
Principal & Head of Advisory Services
Boston, Massachusetts

Afterword

After the credits in *Ferris Bueller's Day Off*, Ferris appears on screen again and says, "You're still here? It's over." As we finished reading all of the submissions and working to put the book together with our publisher, Sarah Hadden (CCI Press), we felt a combination of gratitude and a bit of a letdown; this has been such a great experience. We were inspired daily.

You're at the end of the book, but we think this isn't an end; rather, it's a new chapter.

When we talked about sending the elevator back down at the beginning of the book, we said it was one of our favorite themes, and the willingness to do so is a common thread among the contributors and our community. Many of the authors have sent the elevator back down, and all of us are riding on the elevator. Just like life, the elevator goes up and it goes down, and sometimes it stops on an unexpected floor.

This book is not just about our mentors, advocates, and sponsors (although we have some wonderful ones); it is about our extraordinary community: people in the lobby, on the elevator, on the way up, or sending it back down.

So what's next?

We hope some of these anecdotes and lessons learned resonate with you and that you are inspired. But more than that, we hope that if something strikes a chord, you will reach out to one of the authors here, or someone who has impacted your career, and catch up. We would love the positivity and support we've seen here to flow out into the rest of the world.

Sometimes being in ethics and compliance can feel like a lonely position in an organization. It is rare to hear of an overstaffed E&C function, and there are times when you need to stand up for a principle or position that makes you unpopular. No one ever said this was an easy job.

On the other hand, no professional community is more helpful and more supportive than this one. As E&C practitioners, we have the rare ability to reach out and ask questions, receive guidance, see policies, and share practices with people who may even work for the competition.

At the end of the day, we all want organizations to be ethical and to do the right thing. After all, if one organization has a great idea and someone else can use or adapt it to increase compliance, we are all making everything a little bit better.

So to you, our writers, contributors, supporters, and readers—thank you for being here and being part of this amazing group of people.

And, as Ferris said, "Go home." But don't worry, our community will be here fighting the good fight again tomorrow.

About the Authors

Mary Shirley calls New Zealand home and started her career working there for government regulators in the areas of data privacy and antitrust. Since then, she has become a global citizen and has been based in Singapore (twice), Hong Kong, Dubai, and Boston, assisting global companies to create world-class compliance programs.

Through these international opportunities, Mary caught the travel bug, which she caters to as often as possible—in between creating podcasts with Lisa Fine for the Great Women in Compliance Podcast and her day job as Head of Culture of Integrity and Compliance Education at a multinational health care company. In her current role, Mary splits her time between the company's legal and compliance departments, leading global compliance training and communications initiatives, promoting and measuring a culture of integrity, and facilitating workstreams related to an FCPA monitorship.

Mary spends her time thinking about topics for compliance articles, trying new restaurants with friends (molecular gastronomy? Yes, please!), hosting networking meet-ups in Boston, and wondering which continent she should live on next.

Lisa Fine started her career at an international law firm, where she was a litigator and also led the pro bono program at the firm's Washington, D.C. office. After leaving that role, Lisa worked in public interest law and advocated on behalf of persons with disabilities. In retrospect, these two roles set Lisa on the path to ethics and compliance, as both helped her connect with those who were striving to do the right thing.

Today, Lisa is Director of Compliance at a leading education company, where she serves in the global compliance office and strives to promote an ethical culture internally, including leading anti-bribery and anti-corruption compliance and training, investigations, risk assessments, and third-party due diligence. Prior to this role, Lisa was the Director of Global Compliance at the world's leading airline catering provider.

Lisa is thrilled to co-host the Great Women in Compliance Podcast with Mary and also really enjoys travel adventures and trying new restaurants, sometimes with Mary! Lisa lives in Washington, D.C., with her Havapoo puppy, Rocky, and enjoys spending time with her family and friends, exercising (especially boxing), and visiting the many museums in D.C.

Index

CCI Press is the publishing imprint of CCI Media Group, parent company of Corporate Compliance Insights (CCI). CCI is the web's premier, independent, global source of news and opinion for compliance, ethics, risk, and audit. Founded in 2010, CCI provides a knowledge-sharing forum and publishing platform for established and emerging voices in compliance and ethics, and is a recognized creator, publisher, and syndication source for editorial and multimedia content for today's compliance professional.

Made in the USA
Columbia, SC
25 June 2023

19082371R00100